C000126845

The
Jenkins's's's's's

CHRIS NEEDS

presents

The Jenkins's's's's's

Wales's First Family

Chris Needs: author, creator and custodian of the diaries
Edited by Haydn Price
Associate Editor: Gabe Cameron
Illustrations by Mark Davies

First impression: 2008
© Copyright Chris Needs, Mark Davies and Y Lolfa Cyf., 2008
The text © Copyright 2008 Chris Needs
Illustrations © Copyright 2008 Mark Davies

Names, characters, places and incidents featured in this publication
are either the product of the author's imagination or are used fictitiously.
Any resemblance to actual persons (living or dead), events, or locales,
without satiric intent, is unintentional and purely coincidental. None
of the contents of this publication may be reproduced by any means,
except for purposes of review, without the express written permission of
the author.

Editor: Haydn Price
Associate editor: Gabe Cameron
Cover and illustrations: Mark Davies
Book design: Y Lolfa

To view the continuing weekly saga of The Jenkins's's's's's in comic
strip format, visit: www.friendlygarden.co.uk

ISBN: 978 1 84771 106 9

Published, printed and bound in Wales
by Y Lolfa Cyf., Talybont, Ceredigion SY24 5HE
website www.ylolfa.com
e-mail ylolfa@ylolfa.com
tel 01970 832 304
fax 832 782

Introduction

WELL, WELL, WELL – here we are then: the Jenkins's's's's's!!!!!!!!!!!!!!!

I've been told by the publisher of this book and that plump DJ Chris something, to give you a run down like of my wonderful family.

Well let's start with me, Gladys. I'm Mam, the hub of the household. I keep everything together: money, teenage children and my husband Dai, my little lump of lard he is. I mustn't go off on one. He don't work, in fact he 'ave never worked in his life.

There's my beautiful boy Philllip – as you read on I'm sure you'll agree he's Mammy's little soldier, even if he do 'ave an handbag.

Not forgetting my daughter Shantelll – she 'ave so many boyfriends, she's up and down those stairs day and night. Her feet must be worn out, love her.

Now what about our Idwal? He's the old man upstairs. We're not really sure of his age and I don't think he is either. It's like when someone asks what size shoes he wears. He always answers, "Anything from a 7 to an 11." I reckon he's in his 80s to tell the truth.

Then there's my other son Gareth and his wife, madam Cherylll from sin city. They're always bringing my granddaughter Maxine Roxanne to stay, a real little cow she is.

There's Elsie next door, she's very accommodating. We live in a council semi-detached and she've let us knock through an adjoining door, so that we only pay one TV licence. Mind you, I begrudge paying even 'alf when we could 'ave it for free – if only that Idwal would tell 'em he's over 75 down at that post office.

The rest will become transparent as you do read on like, innit.

Anyway, enjoy my glorious family. I reckon if this was a film and you were watching it in a cinema there wouldn't be a dry seat in the house.

Read on love, read on…

GLADYS

Ponty Pantin News
* WEEK 1 *

WELL, HERE WE ARE: me and my weekly diary of the 'appenings that 'ave 'appened in Ponty Pantin. Things are all front to back as usual. Anyway, here goes…

Monday

I had tumps of washing to do after our 'oliday in Benidorm we 'ave just come back off, thanks to the Social. They makes life worth while. I'm sure our Dai's eye sight is on the blink. He'd put fags in his socks instead of in his plastic bags. There's fags everywhere: in my make up bag, inside my heated rollers, everywhere. I think he should go to that chiropractor to 'ave his eyes seen to.

Idwal upstairs has come over all funny like. Since he's home he's speaking Spanish – he's sticking an 'o' on the end of every word.

Anyway I'd better get my act together a bit sharpish because our Gareth's wife, madam Cherylll from sin city, is coming to pick up our Maxine Roxanne later. Duw, she's a miserable moll. If she smiled her face would crack. I had to buy her something from Spain of course, so I bought her some chocolates, all of them coffee creams. She hates those. Elsie loved the donkey I bought her. She's got it in the toilet and she keeps toilet rolls in the saddle bags. Fabluss.

Our Philll had his friend Simon over last week. He stayed with our Philll in his bedroom on the camp bed I put next to our Philll's bed. Do you know that Simon is a very tidy boy. That camp bed looks like it hasn't been slept in but our Philll's looks like twenty men 'ave been through his.

I 'aven't seen much of Dai, he's out and about wheeling and dealing. He must be working hard and under a lot of strain. He's taken 10 cartons of fags with him. His chest will be bad again, you wait and see.

Tuesday

I've got to tidy the parlour up a bit 'cause our Shantelll is entertaining tonight, some fella from the east called Vladimir. Strange name for Newport that, innit? Hmmm – entertaining? … and her in the family way mind you! Anyway, as long as he's good to her and is willing to pay half the rent, half the food, half the electric and gas, he'll do for me.

Duw, our dog Christopher 'ave missed us. He 'aven't spoke a word to us since we've come back from Spain. I've tried to tempt him with some Asda's ham but he's staying schdwm. Something 'ave rattled his bits I'm telling you. I've noticed that he's put a lot of weight on since he's been staying with Elsie. Something 'ave got into his system. I'd better take him to be seen to by the vet later in the week.

I've got to fill in the form as well for the hardship grant. Well, you've got to look after yourself as best you can 'aven't you? They'll see how hard up we are 'cause I'll use one of those envelopes we nicked from the hotel in Spain. I'll tell them we can't afford to buy our own.

Wednesday

Dai's ready for the off. He's taking some wood to London. I hope he'll be alright in that council van. I would let him use the brand new Renault Clio that we 'ave had for our Idwal's legs, but I don't think he'd get it all in the boot.

Elsie 'ave just been in and told me about a new thing she's got, a black box or something. I told her straight, "I don't like these modern groups. Give me Des O'Connor anytime." I tell you now, if someone broke into her house they'd leave a tenner on the table. Honest to God.

I've just dropped Christopher off at the vet's and he's staying in over night. There's posh for ew, innit? We'll 'ave the results tomorrow.

Shantelll's done OK with this Vladimir, but he don't

sound Newportish to me and his last name ends with off or something. So I told him he'd settle in well, everything ends with off round here.

Anyway, Dai's back soon so I'd better get his favrite tea ready: boil in the bag chicken and mushroom casserole over chips and mash.

Thursday

Dai's still in bed so I've 'phoned the council yard to tell them that he's not coming in today. Duw, I don't know, he'll be cropped again this week. Thank God the Giro is due tomorrow.

Christopher is home I'm glad to say but with some bad news: he's not Christopher but Christine and he's with puppy or should I say puppies. I can't believe it. I'm still going to 'ave to call the dog Christopher, or maybe I shouldn't, people will think he is gay and I couldn't 'ave that in my house.

Anyway, Dai had a bit of a tiring day yesterday. He was supposed to take the wood to London. He stopped in Swindon and asked, "Is this London?" The fella said, "No, keep on going." Then he stopped in Reading and asked, "Is this London?" and another fella said, "No, keep on going." Then he parked right outside Tower Bridge and asked, "Is this London?" and some piece said to him, "Yes," so our Dai says to her, "Where do you want the wood then love?" He's awful helpful mind.

Friday

A fella came to our door and wanted to 'ave the payments for the double glazing we had put in a couple of months ago, so I calls our Dai to see to him. Dai couldn't understand why he wanted payments from us. Dai told him straight, "You said they would pay for themselves in six months." He soon went sharpish when our Philll came down the stairs plucking his eyebrows.

I've broken the news about the dog changing sex while we were away. Shantelll 'ave painted his basket pink so things should sort themselves out from now on.

We are trying to get a stair lift in for our Idwal off the council. Damn it will be handy. It'll save me carrying all those clothes up to the airing cupboard all day.

Saturday

The usual thing: sport all day, Dai back and fore to the betting shop, Shantelll trying on different clothes 'cause we're all going to the Karaoke down the club tonight.

The last time we all went we decided to choose songs for each other, which of course all ended in tears. Shantelll chose 'Stand by your Man' for our Philll and he chose 'The Drinking Song' for her. Of course our Dai sang his song to me, 'Who's Sorry Now?'

I've set the video to record *Bullseye* and I've rinsed the bleach out of the bosh.

I'm really looking forward to tonight. They've got a male stripper down there. Philll's already in the bath.

Sunday

No sign of our Philll, he must 'ave made off with a girl somewhere and Simon's been knocking and 'phoning all morning. Dai's got the usual hangover as big as his belly, Shantelll went and stayed with that eastern fella Vladimir and me, well some things never change. I'm in the kitchen making our favrite Sunday dinner: mince and chips of course.

I hope our Philll is alright. The last time I saw him he was helping that male stripper with his equipment in the van out the back of the club. I warned him mind. I said to him, "Don't you go lifting nothing heavy, you'll 'ave a pain in your back." God he does some queer things on times.

Anyway, I'd better clear away the pots and pans and tidy up a bit. Our new dishwasher is supposed to be coming tomorrow and our new wide screen television and dvd player built in. But there is one problem: where am I going to put the new flat screen computer? God, it's a hard life.

Ponty Pantin News
* WEEK 2 *

WELL HERE WE ARE AGAIN, not 'appy as can be. Dai's done my head in this week, I'll tell you all about it in a moment. Our Philll is a worry to me. I'm sure he's got a girl preggers. I can't think of anything else that's bothering him. Oh and Idwal 'ave had a shot up on the pools.

Monday

Well the computer 'ave come, look, and the new telly. Oh, you should 'ave seen the neighbours nosing something terrible. Dai reckons it's like watching telly through a letter box. I might send it back 'cause the picture 'ave got gaps on the top and bottom. I don't want to miss anything now do I?

We 'ave had some wonderful news. Idwal 'ave won some money on the pools, just over £2,000 and our Shantelll 'ave told him that she needs to 'ave an operation soon and it costs £1,200.

Still 'aven't seen sight of our Philll. That erratic male stripper must 'ave a lot of equipment.

Dai's in court on Thursday, something about working and claiming. Well I've never heard such nonsense. Don't worry, I'm going to court with him. I'll sort it out.

I must 'phone the council soon as our toilet seat 'ave broke in half and it's in three pieces and we can't get BBC 2.

Tuesday

I 'ave had a gutsful of farmer Jones across the road. There's always a racket going on with the cows and geese but this morning that cockerel didn't stop for breath, so I went and told him straight, "If you don't shut that cock up of yours I'll 'ave it for tea."

11

I've 'phoned the council again about the tiles that are missing off the outside toilet. Idwal reckons it could 'ave been some bad wind one night that blew them off.

The water board 'ave been to check my water, it's a funny colour and it's not fit for drinking. I also told the council to mend the garden path 'cause our Shantelll tripped and now she's preggers.

Wednesday

The dishwasher finally turned up. Oh damn it looked smart but it's torture trying to keep Idwal from washing his pants in it. Mind you, I don't mind him washing his teeth in it. Love him.

I'm a bit busy today getting Dai's white shirt ready 'cause he's in court tomorrow. Damn he's had some wear out of it: weddings, funerals, court. You don't get quality like that today do you?

Our Gareth and Cherylll's kitchen floor is damp terrible so I called the council again and told them, "Look here you, our Cherylll's kitchen floor is damp awful. She's got four small children and would like a fifth. So could you send someone round to see to it?"

You'll never guess what. I hears the door going and there he is: Mammy's little soldier, Philll. I looks at him and noticed some red marks on his neck, so I says to him, "I told you so, I told you to put some protection on. Those mossceetoos in Spain 'ave had you terrible." But he's so brave and he's got a wonderful smile on his face.

Mind you I 'ave warned him, "Don't you bring no babies back here." Our Dai is so proud of him. Dai asked the other night, "Where are you off to boy?" Our Philll replied, "I'm off out with the boys Dad." Aw he's ever so good.

Thursday

Off we go to court and they called us in. "Mr Jenkins," the man said. "We 'ave a photo of you in a council van." So I buts in like and says, "Oh Dai, you've been lying to me again. You told me that you were walking everyday like the doctor told you to and you've been having a lift to the job centre with Jason the council every day. Wait till I get you 'ome."

They dismissed the case from lack of evidence and gave Dai a pass for the bus to go into town and increased his Incapacity Benefit, fair play mind.

We gets home to find that Idwal 'ave bought an electric heated chair and it moves up and down automatic like. Which reminds me, years ago when my mother was alive our Dai said he'd love to buy her a chair and was really looking forward to plugging it in. Oh, he's a darling.

Friday

I've just 'phoned the council again. I told them our toilet is blocked and I can't bath our Maxine Roxanne until it 'ave been cleared. Nobody cares do they?

Simon looks down mind you. He must 'ave terrible hay fever. He 'ave just come out of our Philll's room and if I didn't know better I'd say he'd been crying. I told him not to put his fags in his back pocket otherwise they'd be all bent.

I've noticed that the male stripper 'ave been back and fore to see our Philll. I'm sure he wants to offer him something and I 'ave to admit our Philll has got a lovely little figure. But that Simon just can't get a look in, so me, dull as hell innit, goes out the back and picks him some pansies to give to his mother. That'll cheer him up.

Saturday

We decides to go for an outing, so we puts it to the vote and Barry Island it is! I cut a pile of sandwiches: plum jam, corned beef and marmite. Fabluss, so off we goes. I picked our Maxine Roxanne up on the way and made off to Barry.

Philll didn't want to come, he wanted to watch his favrite film on TV: *Sleepless in Seattle*.

Idwal has spent some money on us mind. Fish and chips, bingo and a bag of pennies for us all to go on the fruit machines. Lush.

I don't know why people go abroad when you've got places

like this. You can even get cheap booze and fags. Malcolm the taxis gets loads.

We headed home and collapsed straight away. What a cracking day.

Sunday

The vicar came to see our Shantelll about having the baby baptised when she's had it. They were talking away in the parlour and the next thing, out comes the vicar and asks to use the bathroom. I told him that we'd had a bit of trouble with the one upstairs and said he could use the one out the back. So off he scoots. I asked him if he wanted a newspaper, but he declined.

Anyway, a bit later when he comes out he says to me, "Gladys, there's no lock on the toilet door." So I says to him, "Don't worry vicar, we 'aven't had a bucket of caca pinched in 20 years."

Ponty Pantin News
* WEEK 3 *

WELL HELLO MY LOVES, it's Gladys here again with my weekly diary and believe you me, this week is no exception. Dai's brother Willy is out of clink, apparently he was done as a get away driver, but he swears to this day that he got into the wrong car. He 'aven't got the gift of the gab like me.

Monday

Well we had a right good shock on Monday morning. There it was in the paper: 'Willy Jenkins is released'. I couldn't get over it. I bet he'll make his way by here for starters. I'll 'ave to super glue the ornaments to the mantle piece.

The dog Christopher/Christine 'ave had three lovely puppies, one of each we think. One is called Antonio after Antonio Banderas, one is called Madonna after that singing piece with a gap in her teeth and the other one is going to be called Larry, after Larry Grayson. Fabs.

We had a lovely tea today: faggots. Our Philll loves 'em, and of course straight after tea it's a ritual we watch *Wales Today* with that Jamie Owen. Ooh our Philll loves him, he says he could look at his voice for hours.

Tuesday

I don't know if I told you before but I've got a sister living in Australia, Nancy, and our Philll loves her to bits, well so much in fact that he's got a new email name now: Nancy Boy. Aww, he must miss her a lot.

We 'ave talked about sending him out there to Australia – Philll 'ave always said that he would love to go into Sydney. He was always good at geography in school.

Elsie 'ave had a new frock from that new posh shop in

Ponty called Elle. I think you spell it Elle. Apparently she asked her fancy man if she could 'ave a new frock from town and he asked how much, and when she said £360 he said, "Go to 'ell." So she did. Damn she looks nice in it.

Anyway there's a knock on the door so I tells our Dai to get his stick just in case it's the Social and lo and behold, there he stands large as life: our Dai's brother Willy Jenkins's's's's's. So I calls him in. To cut a long story short, I 'ave let him stay until he gets a housing association flat.

Wednesday

Elsie fell outside, cut her head, cut her knee and twisted her ankle she did. Ooh she was landed, chuffed. She was straight on the 'phone to a solicitor to make a claim. I've never seen her so happy.

I 'ave offered our Dai's Willy to sleep in that camp bed with our Philll but he's declined, it must be our Philll's snoring.

Idwal is upstairs laying on the bed with a plate full of chickling, strings of it. Oh, he loves it.

Philll came and spoke to me and told me that he fancied an Italian, so I says to him, "Don't worry love, that's not a problem for Mam." So I nips up the Co-op and gets him a tiggly taggly.

The house seems to be getting smaller: there's boxes everywhere, something to do with our Dai's Willy. He's storing a few things for a friend, love him. I 'aven't got the heart to say no.

Thursday

Our Shantelll 'ave a little job delivering leaflets for the Co-op – 4,000 of them. Damn she's a good little worker: it only took her 15 minutes, all done!

Oh it's a good job that I was looking out of the window, there's the ashman collecting rubbish and he's laughing like hell with our Shantelll. I wonder if he's the father of her baby. Duw, I can't get over how quick she 'ave delivered those leaflets.

Friday

We're off to a fancy dress ball tonight up the club. It's one of Idwal's old friend's birthday, so I'm going as Carmen Miranda. I've borrowed Elsie's plastic fruit from next door and stuck it on my old chapel hat. Shantelll is going as Madonna and so is Philll. Dai, oooh damn he's clever, he's put a piece of sandpaper hanging from the crutch of his trousers, he's said he's going as a rough handful. There's line dancing up the club as well, our Philll loves that tune 'Ride 'em Cowboy'. That's his favrite.

Three lovely boys called to see our Dai's Willy, we had a lovely chat, they offered to get me anything I wanted. What was their names now? Oh yes, I remember: Strip Jack, Fiddler and Norman the Nutter. Ooh damn they were lovely lads. I hope they call again, you don't see many good folk around like that nowerdays do you?

Ponty Pantin News
* WEEK 4 *

WELL HELLO MY LOVELIES. I hope you are all alright. Well let me tell you now, this week has been epic what with Willy staying and Spanish men running about in the night naked. Anyway, I'd better get on with it. Here goes...

Monday

Me and our Shantelll were outside the house near the farm across the road and there was a calf being born. I said to our Shantelll, "Look at that little cow by there." Shantelll says back to me, "I know Mam. I've never liked his wife at all."

Mind you, our Philll went to see the specialist last Saturday, apparently to 'ave a check up. I don't know why he had to take a phrase book with him. Anyway, off he goes and there was an East German woman specialist there in the hospital to see to him. She looked at his eyes and then she checked his heart and then his ears, but right at the end she got the rubber glove out with some gel on it and put it where the sun don't shine. She asked him, "Am I hurting you, Mr Jenkins?" Our Philll replied, "Can I call you Simon?" He was never any good with names.

Tuesday

Willy, that's our Dai's brother who is just out of clink, is still staying with us and there's more boxes than ever clogging up my passageway. I told him that he'd 'ave to shift the boxes because Shantelll's pen friend Rapheal is coming to stay soon.

Idwal is upstairs on the bed eating his favrite chickling and our Dai's downstairs with his favrite: stuffed hearts.

Wednesday

Rapheal turns up with his brother Paco in tow and what good-looking boys, dark tanned, no hair on their chests. Our Shantelll was around them non-stop and so was our Philll, he just wants to learn Spanish see.

Shantelll's let Paco sleep on the floor in her room, she's only got a single bed. They could never fit in that little bed, he'd find it awfully hard, love him, and he's such a good boy, he's given me some money towards his keep.

All of a sudden, our Idwal starts speaking in Spanish to Rapheal. He said, "Muchas grathias, appendage." I said to our Idwal, "What does that mean?" And he translated it straight away. "It means," he said, "Thank you very much, cock." Rapheal seemed lovely but not a patch on Jamie Owen. His body's a chapel.

Our Philll's friend Simon looks a bit down again. I told him straight, "You looks a bit queer love. You could do with something hot inside you." Better if he found a nice little wife to cook for him.

Thursday

Idwal is making a will. I know, I've had a peep at it. He's leaving his false teeth to his mate Maldwyn up the centre and all of his frozen chickling to Dai. Mind you, I can't see him going for a good while 'cause he's got a policy for a private hospital – BLIPA or something like that. He said he couldn't wait to be bad to go in there. "Gorgeous place," he said.

Mind you, when Elsie next door lost her husband she went to the newspaper to put a piece in, like you do. She said to the man, "I'd like to put something in the obituary," and the bloke said to her, "What would you like to write madam?" She said, "Fred is dead." The bloke in the newspaper office said to her, thinking she must be short of money, "This week is buy one get one free, you get six words for the price of three." So Elsie said, "Fred is dead – Volvo for sale."

Friday

That Rapheal has been sleep-walking. He's been traipsing across the landing into our Philll's room every night. I hope he doesn't wake our Philll, otherwise he'll get his dander up.

I've been a bit pushed with feeding them all and to be honest I didn't want to let the side down so I told Dai to say that he's not hungry and then I'd 'ave enough food to go round.

So there we are sat at the table and I says to our Dai, "Would you like some dinner love?" Our Dai like a true trooper said, "No love, I'm not hungry."

Anyway they cleared the lot and our Dai had none. Next thing, I brings out a massive apple crumble and I says to Dai, "Would you like some apple crumble love?" Dai says, "Yes please." So I says to him, "Well you can't 'ave none. You never ate your dinner."

Saturday

Willy and Dai 'ave gone to the bookies. Rapheal is teaching our Philll some Spanish upstairs. He must be teaching him Spanish dancing, there's a lot of banging going on and poor Shantelll looks lost. Anyway in the evening we all goes up the club and on the way our Philll fell in a puddle of water and was soaked. He said, "Never mind Mam. I'll take my trousers off and go to the club in my boxer shorts. They're quite trendy."

Well when we gets to the club there's a queue to get in and we were waiting over 20 mins outside, so me being chopsy, I says to the doorman, "Hey it's cold out here, we're freezing and our Philll 'ave just come in his shorts."

Duw, some people got no heart.

Sunday

Nobody moved on Sunday morning: everyone was knackerated.

But there's me getting on with it, starting the dinner and of course washing our Philll's trousers. Well, talking of Mammy's little soldier, I went up the stairs 'cause I could hear noises coming from our Philll's room: Ah, ah, ahhhhh.

Well, I thought, what's going on in here? 'ave he brought a girl back? So I enters and there he was sat on the bed and do you know what he said to me? "Ah ah, help get the top off this bottle of pop Mam." Oh he's like a sledge.

Then all of a sudden the 'phone went. It was Elsie next door and she said to me, "Well you'll never guess who 'ave died?" I says no and she says to me, "Go and light a fag. I've got a list." God she knows everything that goes on in this village.

I've warned our Dai to cut down on his drinking. Mind you, I shouldn't complain, he's down to 12 pints a night. He's got the runs, you know, the 'back door gallops' and I'm awful worried about him. So he went to the doctor's the other day and he asked our Dai about his bowels and Dai, trying not to be rude said, "Well doc, one day I can paint the walls and the next I can bolt the door with it." He's good with words mind.

Rapheal is thinking of stopping on for a while longer, he really gets on well with our Philll and his English has improved proper tidy. In fact he sounds as if he comes from here sometimes. He's picked up a lot of handy phrases like 'I'm before you butt' and 'Don't you call my wife a piece'.

Well the baby is due in the next few weeks and our Shantelll 'ave decided on names. If it's a boy it's going to be John Wayne Jenkins and if it's a girl, Chantilly Lace Jenkins. So classy.

Anyway I'm gonna do my best to cure our Dai from the runs. I'll put a bit extra Bisto in his gravy. That'll thicken it.

Ponty Pantin News
* WEEK 5 *

HIYA LOVES. GLADYS HERE with the 'appenings that 'ave 'appened again this week.

Rapheal is still here and getting on like a house on fire with our Philll. Shantelll 'ave got the blues. The baby's due in a few weeks and we still don't know who the father is. Well put it this way, we know the eight it's not. Anyway, here goes...

Monday

Went into Elsie's for a cuppa and she was under the stairs throwing dust on the top of the gas meter. I asked her what she was doing and she told me that she was due a meter reading in the next few days. Strange for her not to keep it clean.

Anyway I wasn't there five minutes and the door bell went. Lovely bell, it plays the Welsh National Anthem: 'My hen laid a haddock'. She was right, it was the gas man and under the stairs he went. She said, "Oh if I knew you were coming I would 'ave put the duster around love." God, she's a strange woman. I don't know how he could concentrate. She was showering him with Welsh cakes and biscuits and she cut up a Swiss Roll as well, and I had been offered nothing.

Anyway he soon went and Elsie seemed to calm down at last. God that house is awful hot. I must change to gas, it's much cheaper. Elsie's bills are only around £16 a quarter.

So anyway, I goes back in next door and Philll and that Rapheal are still in bed, so up I goes to wake them and do you know they were in bed together, love them. I know they are only trying to save on my washing.

Tuesday

Got my jewellery out to clean it up a bit and I noticed that the gold-plated necklace Dai bought me 20 years ago has started to fade and go black. I must take it back and complain.

I'm going up the solicitors a bit later on after with our Idwal, he wants me to see to his testimonials. I told him that's a job for BLIPA, not the solicitor.

With that there's a 'phone call from our Shantelll. She was in the £1 shop in town buying things for the baby and she thought her waters had broken but it was only a bottle of pop that had spilt down her front. I asked her where she was ringing from and she said from her knickers to her ankles. She's twp.

Elsie is having an insurance assessor around because all her carpets 'ave been ruined with bleach right through the house. Strange really because normally she can't open the bottle, I've got to do it for her. Maybe our Dai's Willy opened it: he seems to be in there a lot. He's full of helpful ideas mind.

Wednesday

Dai 'ave not gone into work today, broken flask, so I've got him around me now and I wants to get on with my housework. Then he says to me, "Gladys, you've worked hard enough. I'm taking you out down the club. There's a special show on this afternoon."

I was landed, so off we scoots down the club and as soon as we got there Dai nipped off to the bookies. So in I goes and what do you think is on? There's a male stripper again, so I thought, well there's no harm in having a peep and in I goes and who was there? Our Philll and Rapheal in the front row and about 300 women.

The stripper was called Tarzan Boy and he only had a little loin cloth on and there were six electric fans around the dance floor. Every time he stood near one, one of the fans would blow his loin cloth right up. He'd better be careful, he could catch a chill. Anyway, four of the women got up and two sat on his arms and two sat on his legs, but after that I couldn't see what was going on. There was a que all around him. He must 'ave been selling cds. Anyway not to worry, Elsie was up there on stage, so she'll tell me later.

Thursday

It's Elsie's turn to come in to our house for a cuppa, but she never turned up. Strange I thought, we never miss Jamie Owen on the wireless at 11 o'clock. So in I goes, like a cow at the gate and Elsie comes to the door. "What's the matter?" I asks, and Elsie's got her hand over her mouth. "What's up with you Else?" I says again. She says to me, "I've lost my teeth." So I tells her straight, "You had too much to drink in the club yesterday, you silly woman. You won't get another pair of false teeth on the NHS now you've blown that."

I'm sure our Dai's brother Willy 'ave been in a prison hospital. He've still got the identification thing on, funny mind why they've put it on his leg and not his wrist. He says it irritates his wrist, so I suppose it makes sense.

Anyway I got a fabluss tea for us today: cawl. I goes to the butcher and gets bones for our dog Christopher/Christine. Duw, it makes a lovely stock.

Our Willy's been buying a bit of grub as well. I've got so much milk and we're having milky coffee every night.

Friday

There's a knock on the door and there's someone collecting for that children's charity, what do you call them, Ban Ade Does. I told them straight, "There's two in here for a start, take them with pleasure."

I hadn't shut the door two mins when it went again and there was the police asking if I had had any milk pinched off the door. I told them straight, "Ours comes from the Co-op."

That Caprice next door, on the other side, she really thinks she's the bee's ankles. She's always parading around in new frocks. Cow dressed as calf if you ask me. I really can't stand her. She's like the north sea: deep, cold and nobody drills there anymore. Mind you, I couldn't help but feel sorry for her. She'd told me she'd broken her arm in three places. I told her straight not to go them three places again.

Saturday

We're all off to Cardiff today to do a bit of shopping. Our Dai's sister Slybil, we call her Slab for short, lives there in a very upmarket place, lower Adamsdown. Beautiful.

Philll said that he couldn't stay with us all day because him and Simon and Rapheal are going to something or other called Mardi Gras. Oh, I've always loved those small peas.

Anyway, we goes into our Slab's house, she 'ave cladding on the front of her house, all pink and gorgeous. She always gives us a welcome. Mind you, I do feel sorry for her because her husband Cledwyn ran off with another man. I'm glad our Dai's not like that. What would people say in our village? But there you are, it 'appens. We asked her if she wanted to come to St David's Hall to see Julian Clary but she didn't seem fussed on that idea.

So off we all goes into Cardiff and I love that big posh shop, Debanams's's's's's and we did a tidy bit of shopping and then we meet our Philll in a lovely pub called the Leather Trousers. Philll and the boys had Babychams and me, Dai and Slab had a pint of Dark each. Lovely. Gagging we were.

Then all of a sudden a fella started talking to our Dai and asked him to go upstairs with him. I said for a laugh, "Go on Dai." We'd had a few mind. I said, "If you don't like it make a noise like an animal and we'll come and get you and if you do like him sing a song." Anyway, Dai goes upstairs with this flussy fella and we were killing ourselves laughing. All of a sudden I could hear, "Moo...Moo...Moo...Moon River." Don't think we'll ever go there again mind!

Sunday

No sign of the boys. I hope they bring those Mardi Gras peas home in time for our dinner. Dai's a little bit sheepish about what 'appened down that whatsaname bar in Cardiff. It 'ave made his gout play up.

Shantelll wants to 'ave a go at a paella to impress Rapheal. I think he'll love that: chickens, cockles and muscles. Our Idwal is upstairs and I daren't disturb him while Dewi Griffiths is on the wireless.

We had a beautiful dinner and we've kept the bones to make soup tomorrow.

Tonight I'm filling in a form to 'ave a cleaner's job up the club. I've started it already: eyes – two; sex – occasionally; hobbies – bingo, knitting and skittles. That'll impress the committee.

Gladys

Ponty Pantin News
* Week 6 *

HOW BE DARLINGS? IT'S Gladys here again with the 'appenings that 'ave 'appened here in Ponty Pantin. Dai's taking us to the zoo, God knows if we'll notice the difference. Poor Shantelll is ready to give birth and a day at the zoo will do her good. Idwal, well, he is just the same and for me, life gets harder by the day, what with the housework and looking after them all. I'll be glad when Philll settles down with a nice girl and gives me a break.

Monday

Washing day today. I'm so glad we had the new washing machine with the hardship grant off the Social. It spins a treat. I've even tossed a salad in it. Fabluss.

I've put our Dai's trousers in for a wash but you'll never guess what I've done. I washed the Social book and it's in pieces. I'll 'ave to get our Dai to go down and get a new one this afternoon after he finishes work. He wasn't too pleased about it because he had a chance of a fiddle down the yard, but off he went.

Dai got to the Social office in our new mobility car. I went in the boot and got the stick out and in he went, limping awful he was. Anyway, out he comes and said there would be a new one in the post. He didn't drop me in it. He said he'd peed himself and the book was ruined. They gave him a form to fill in for new trousers. Tidy.

Tuesday

We're off to the zoo today and we're all excited. We gets in the car with sandwiches, flasks and pop and off we goes.

We had to stop for Idwal to go to the toilet six times and

Shantelll eight times but they say that every cloud has a silver lining. I was glad to open the door every couple of miles what with Dai letting off terrible after eating them four breasts of lamb last night.

We gets to the zoo eventually and Philll started straight away, "Mammy, I want to feed the animals." So I grabs a zoo keeper and says, "Can my little boy feed the animals?" and fair do's he said, "Yes, he can feed the birds." When our Philll went in to feed them they were all dead on the floor with their legs stuck up in the air. "Never mind," said Dai to him. "Feed them to the lions. Waste not want not."

There was some lovely animals in the zoo and we had some nice photos as well. Shantelll had her photo taken holding a monkey, well it's good practice for her for when she has the baby. And Philll had a photo taken of him holding a snake. God, he wasn't frightened at all, in fact he handled it so well I could swear he had done it before.

I said to our Dai, "Look at these lovely flowers. Geraniums and chrysanthemums and look at those lovely pansies over there." Philll disappeared when I said that. He must be allergic to pansies.

We gets home in the night in time to catch the club for bingo. I had a £2 line and Idwal won the raffle: a book on wine making. God help us all!!!!!

Wednesday

I had to do a bit of food shopping and fair play our Dai's brother Willy has given me £100 as he does every week. Our Shantelll came with me, she always finds the bargains.

We gets to the supermarket and I saw Shantelll doing something with the price labels. "Look Mam," she says to me. "Cooked chickens 10p each." I blame the printers, there's not enough sticky on them labels. Thank God for people like our Shantelll, in fact she went round the whole store putting the prices back on the items. I think she was hoping for a job there, love her.

There was a special offer on tins of corned beef, 15p each and a big tin of Quality Road chocolates was only 36p. Damn, our Shantelll has an eye for a bargain. We came out loaded and I only spent £4.76.

I fancy our Shantelll has got bigger today. She must be ready to drop and in fact she did drop when we got to the car: two bottles of Bacardi. I said, "Shantelll, where did you get them?" She said, "They were in my coat from yesterday. They're a present for our Philll." Aw, she's such an angel, thoughtful to a fault.

Thursday

Dai's gone to the bookies. That'll give me a break, mind you, last week he had a win and fair play he gave me half. I can't complain.

Rapheal is looking forward to seeing snow, well they never get it out there in Spain do they? Philll kept telling him we'll 'ave snow tomorrow, tons of it. "You wait and see. I bet there'll be nearly a foot of it." Oh Rapheal was so excited. Well, I thinks to myself, we'll see!!!!!!

Idwal 'ave ordered himself some new wardrobes from MI5 and our Shantelll is off into hospital today. I think they are going to seduce the baby, that's all she's been saying. I hope they don't give her a Serbian suction, love her, after all it's her first.

Friday

Rapheal gets up first thing to see the snow and of course, there was none. He looked so disappointed and I felt real sorry for him. So I says to our Philll, "That boy looks awful down, you shouldn't 'ave promised him eight inches yesterday."

Anyway, we forgets about the snow, but Dai's got it into his head about a camping 'oliday so he goes to the camping shop to see how much a tent would be. So we all goes for a nose and in went me and Dai while Shantelll and the boys stayed outside.

Shantelll insisted on taking a photo of Philll and Rapheal

outside the tent shop. She's got one of these instant cameras. So she took a lovely photo of the two boys and you can see the sign above them, 'CAMP ARE US'. Damn, she takes a lovely photo.

I'm awful worried about our Idwal. He's got terrible flem. He said it was so bad last week he could plait it. I know what will cure him, some of Elsie's brawn. She makes it in a rabbit mold. That'll do him a power of good.

There's a good film on tonight so I'm staying into watch it. It's called *Carry on up the Khyber*. I like programmes about the human body.

Saturday

Idwal reckons he's taking so many tablets he's gonna leave his body to Mothercare as a rattle. Fair play, he's been bad under the doctor for a while now. Anyway, he's off to town to buy something or other that will change our lives forever.

Elsie is having a bit of a do in her house tonight. It's her birthday. I've got her a card, a stinking one with a fella on the front with nothing on. She'll love it and I've got her a fabluss present, a case of Diamond White, she's such a good neighbour.

Anyway, Idwal marches in with a load of boxes, as if I 'aven't got enough of them with our Dai's Willy. "What's in the boxes Id?" I asked. Do you know what was in them? A wine making kit. I might 'ave known. Anyway, upstairs he goes unpacking everything. God knows what he'll brew up, but he reckons whatever the first brew is, he's gonna call it 'Idwal's Liquour'.

We went into Elsie's later on that evening and she'd prepared a fabluss spread: cocktail pasties and sausage rolls from the Co-op, Spam sandwiches and a fabluss clonk of cheese in the middle. She also had a lovely birthday cake, a real nice one. There was 21 candles on it. Well, there was on my slice anyway. She downed the case of Diamond Whites and four flagons of Dark. She was minging but damn it was a good night.

Sunday

Slab's coming up for Sunday dinner today so I'm doing my best to find enough plates that match. I found a dozen, they all said Castle Bingo on them. Fabluss.

I do miss that Jamie Owen, I wish he was on the wireless on a Sunday. Our Philll sits next to the wireless drooling over him. I'm sure that Philll wants to be a presenter.

Anyway, we sits around the table. We had to use the pasting table to get us all in like and I told our Dai to say Grace, he's good like that. What was the one he said now, oh yes: "Thank you for the Social, it really makes us happy, we'll try to eat the food this week, cos last week it was crappy." Oh he loves to pull my leg.

We played some records after dinner. Philll was in charge of the music. He loves that tune 'YMCA'. We've saved some dinner for Shantelll 'cause she's in hospital. Malcolm the taxis will nip it down for her and her colour mini telly and her mp3 player and her mobile 'phone. I hope this baby comes soon. Philll can't wait to be an aunty. Oh he's a boy.

Dai's brother has just walked in with a new microwave. He said it fell off the back of a lorry. Funny, I thinks to myself, I can't see a dent in it anywhere.

Ponty Pantin News
* WEEK 7 *

WELL HELLO MY LOVES, it's Gladys here with the doings that 'ave 'appened here in Ponty Pantin once again. Philll has taken up sport and Dai's on a diet. Shantelll is still hanging on, love her, and me, well nothing much changes for me. But this week I'm off to do something new and I'm looking about for a cheap 'oliday as well. We like to go four times a year if we can get enough out of the Social.

Monday

Washing day and tumps of it, but I'm landed with the new microwave that Dai's Willy has bought for me. I asked him for the guarantee and he said they don't do them anymore, he said it was just as easy to pick another one up straight away.

Philll, Simon and Rapheal are taking up rugby. They're off down the docks as hookers, mind you they are going to ruin their leather trousers in the mud. They've got no sense, mind you, that Rapheal has made a lot of new friends. There's boys back and fore all times of the day asking for him, so many they'll 'ave to make an appointment so he can fit them all in.

We're off this afternoon to see our Shantelll down the hospital and I feel sorry for her, she's had an infection in her averies. Anyway, we gets to the hospital and in we goes to see our Shantelll and damn I must admit she's settled in well. Home from home. She's got the mini colour telly we had off the catalogue and her mobile 'phone and her Walkman to listen to Jamie Owen on the BBC. She's got her tongs for her hair and loads of electronic games – one was called fast, medium or slow, but she'd worn the battery out on that one.

As we were leaving, this lovely male nurse named Arthur came up to me and asked to pass a message on to Philll on a piece of paper. It said, "A friend of mine is calling in tonight, so it's best that you don't come. Ha ha! Best wishes, Martha." That boy can't spell, love him, must be disletrix.

We had a lovely tea today: chips and gravy, thank goodness for them gravy granals.

Tuesday

I've had a letter back from Radio Wales saying that they can't find that tune I was looking for, for me and Dai's anniversary coming up next month. What's it go like now? "By the rivers of Benidorm, where we got drunk." I thought the BBC would 'ave had that one.

With that there's a knock on our front door and there's a blokie there with spanners and drills and all sorts of things handy like. He asked for Dai, so I said, "Oh he's not here love. He's gone to BLIPA for some treatment on his incurable bad back." So he said he would call later on in the evening. I daren't 'ave told him that Dai was working, he might 'ave been a pimp.

With that in comes the boys loaded with cash. "Where 'ave you been?" I says to them. "We've been on a mission Mam," Philll said, "and there's £150 for you." Well, I was landed, he must 'ave won the rugby, they must 'ave been betting. Mind you, rugby is a hell of a rough game. As he was going up the stairs he shouted down, "Mam 'ave you got any Germoline?" Oh these chaps are terrible, love him.

Dai came in from work and I said to him, "There's been a fella here looking for you and he had a lovely set of tools on him."

Wednesday

Still no news from Shantelll. She must be feeling bunged up stuck in that hospital, but life goes on. I'm putting our Dai on a diet, none of his clothes fit him and it's difficult enough to find big sizes down the charity shop. So I've prepared a special tea for him today: salad, rice and peeled apples with spotted dick and custard for afters and a tray of faggots for supper.

I've just nipped into Ponty to look for a cheap 'oliday so I was nosing through. There was quite a few. Amsterdam: interesting but I don't think Philll would like that, there's only a load of dykes there and you never get the sun. There was a 'oliday in Poland, now Shantelll would love that, she was going to be a Pole dancer before she got preggers.

While I was in the travel shop I met Mrs Dunne. Duw, I 'aven't seen her for yonks. I said to her, "How's your daughter Nellie?" She said, "Don't talk to me about her. She's in London WC something and she 'aven't written to me in three months." I told her that our Dai's Willy is off to London tomorrow and she asked me would Willy look her daughter up and tell her to write. I said of course.

Thursday

Dai's brother Willy has gone to London today and I told him to look out for Mrs Dunne's daughter Nellie in WC something and tell her to write to her mother.

Idwal is playing up again. He's after this piece from up the estate and I must tell you she's been about. She've had more men than the Grand Old Duke of York. She's trying to play hard to get and she'll only conoodle with Idwal if they got engaged and then married. Mind you, Idwal told her to sling her hook. He said, "It's like having a bike for Xmas and you can't ride it till Easter." I'm glad that's knocked on the head. She was only after his money that he won.

Still no news on Shantelll, but the rest will do her good. Before she was preggers she used to 'ave loads of different men to the house. She was up and down those stairs all day, her feet must 'ave been killing her.

I'm thinking about taking up French. Well in this day and age it's awful handy, what with back and fore on fag runs, innit?

Friday

Willy's back from London and let me tell you what 'appened. He got to London and was looking for Mrs Dunne's daughter Nellie, who lives in WC something and what do you think he did? He saw a sign with WC on it and went straight into a ladies toilet, knocked on the toilet door and said, "Are you Nellie Dunne?" She said to him, "Yes, but there's no paper." So Willy said, "Well that's no excuse for not writing to your mother." Mrs Dunne will be so pleased.

Elsie 'ave had a brilliant idea. She wants to knock a hole between the two houses and put in an adjoining door. She reckons that we'll be able to share a telly license then and it will be handy to nip back and fore in the winter. I'll speak to our Dai and see if he can apply for a door between the two houses on the Social. We could say that Elsie was looking after him 'cause of his incurable bad back.

Willy 'ave had a load of sun beds, so he's going to open a sun bed centre in the village. There's an old cafe that's closed down, that might be the ideal place to set it up. It's a pity that Shantelll isn't here, she could 'ave had a load of paint from that council bloke she was knocking around with. Timing has never been her best asset.

Saturday

There was the doorbell going like the clappers. The tent has arrived, the one that Dai ordered from the camp shop. "Where would you like it Mrs?" the man asked. I thought to myself, if I was 20 years younger I'd tell him to take it round the back. But I said, "Take it round the front. I want the neighbours to see." Well you've got to keep up with the Jones's's's's's 'aven't you? The fella seemed quite nice and he made a noise as well so that everybody would 'ave a gawk.

I said to our Philll as he was coming down the stairs, "Do you fancy going camping love?" He looked at me daft. God, he's a queer boy on times. So the tent has been put away, God knows where we'll end up going with it.

We're all going to bingo tonight to see if we can win the national. I'd love a win. I could do with some new clothes. Mind you, talking of clothes, Philll and Rapheal 'ave had new suits, rubber. I don't mind in the least – anything that saves me on ironing will do me love.

Off we went to the bingo and I told our Idwal to go and get six dinners, old age of course. I freezes them and it's cheap and I get to use the plates at home as well.

We hadn't sat down two minutes when they stopped the bingo and announced, "Would Mrs Gladys Jenkins and family go to the manager's office." I thought, oh no, they've caught our Dai working, but it was only our Shantelll on the 'phone wanting some laxatives to see if she could shift the baby. I told her, "Shantelll, you've made me miss a house." I said not to worry and that we'd be up to see her tomorrow. Duw, I don't know. I think Philll will 'ave a baby before her. She's hanging on to it well, poor dab.

Sunday

At 6am the 'phone went, the hospital. "Mrs Jenkins," this piece said, "your daughter has just gone into labour." I thought, what a time to be talking about politics, then I realised what she meant. Mornings aren't a good time for me.

So we all goes up. Idwal in his long johns, me in my overall, Dai in his vest and Philll and Rapheal in their rubber suits. They must 'ave thought it was the *Rocky Horror Show* walking in the hospital. A doctor asked who the father was and Dai said, "I am." The doctor looked dull at us. I can't think why. Anyway, Shantelll had the baby, a baby boy, and all is well.

Philll is trying for a job and he wants to be a managing director. So I tells him, "If you want to do well and 'ave job satisfaction you 'ave to start at the bottom and work your way up to it, otherwise you'll end up with a bum job." So anyway, our Philll and Rapheal 'ave decided to start their own business. They've put a piece in the paper: 'We can fill your delights – got a bad back? We'll sort it out.'

I think they call them ciropratters, anyway they've turned the garage into a surgery and they've got all the gear in there: leather bed, doctors and nurses outfits and mirrors on the ceiling. I hope they do well, it'll keep them off the streets. It might be an idea to send our Dai in with his bad back.

A New Beginning
* WEEK 1 *

SORRY LOVES BUT I'VE been too busy to pen my memoirs for the past few weeks. It really has been hectic 'ere in sun kissed Ponty Pantin.

The committee at the club was insistent that I had the best credentials for the job an' I was successful. I am now the deputy house keeper – well, I am actually the cleaner and double up to collect the glasses when they've got functions on.

Those Golden Garden Girls on that Chris Needs' wireless show had some funny ideas when we asked for suggestions for naming our Shantelll's little darlin. I could swear they were the same names they suggested for that Gabe's pet monkey. Anyway, our Shantelll wanted somethink sophisticated and Welsh so she went with Cadwalider – oooh, ever so posh.

But what with working, helping out with the new baby, cleaning up after Christopher/Christine and the puppies (and our Idwal) I've just been too exhausted.

Mind you, we've extra money coming in as our Philll's surgery is such a success. Just as well as I've another mouth to feed. Raphael's brother Paco was sent over from Spain by his mam and his dad to check up on him an' he's only gone and decided to stay as well.

Now it appears that that Paco and our Shantelll got acquainted on one of our Social trips last year. I am now convinced that Paco maybe the real dad to our Cadwalider. We'll just have to wait until he starts talking; if it comes out in Spanish I'll know I'm right!

Well our Christopher's pups have been playing havoc in the 'ouse, chewing up all our best oil cloth an' all. So I banished them to the back yard where they started to ambush our Philll's clients as they were leaving his clinic. Our Philll's treatments must be good. I've never seen so many gentlemen recover from bad backs as they leapt over the fence into Elsie's. Jones the farmer opposite has offered to take them in – the puppies that is, but we have decided to keep them. For the time being at least! Mind you they'd be good company for that wife of his – same disposition as her!

You'll never guess what that little so and so Shantelll 'ave gone and done? She's getting married to Paco, our Rapheal's butch brother from Spain, and they've decided to get married on Friday this week. Can you believe it? Never mind, leave it to Mam…

Saturday

There's all hell let loose in our house. Shantelll came down the stairs and said, "Mam, me and Paco are getting married." Well, I couldn't believe it. So I says, "Where do you want to get married?" She said to me, "Down our chapel." I thinks to myself, boy, if ever I needed a painting grant off the social it's now!!!

Mind you, Paco wants to take her to Sardenesia for the honeymoon, but our Shantelll said to me, "Is that where they make sardines, Mam?" She's dull as a brush. Shantelll's called the baby Cadwalider and told me she wants to 'ave his ear pierced, like to go with his biker's jacket.

Paco is going to get a job here, he's been offered one down the Co-op. There's so much opportunity here in Ponty Pantin.

Popped in to Elsie's – she's good with a sewing machine – to see if she'll run up a few things for me and to check if she'll 'ave the good coffee for the week.

Anyway, down I goes to see the minister and as luck would 'ave it, he agreed to marry them on Friday. I'm glad he's agreed, I don't fancy going to the registry office down sin city.

Shantelll wants a white wedding and she wants a dress to be remembered. Philll said he'd work on that one, he's got so many contacts now he's opened a surgery. He said he had a dressmaker down there the other day. Bad backs are so common these days.

Anyway, we'll 'ave the reception up the club. The steward told us that we can put the food on top of the pool table and he'd put a few balloons up as well. I tell you now, I'm dreading this week.

Sunday

I'm working up the club cleaning, £4 an hour, no questions asked and all the rubber gloves I can use. Fabluss. I've got to be honest I'm a little put out with the club – with all the hardships and famine in the world they're still putting pineapple chunks in the wee wee basins in the gents. Such a waste, I could 'ave made a lovely trifle with them. I've taken two ashtrays and some beer mats for the house: they'll look tidy on the sideboard.

I thought it best if we all went to chapel today because of the wedding. Well you've got to show willing 'aven't you? I don't want anyone insinerating that we use anyone.

Idwal's going to wear his medals for the wedding and my other son Gareth is taking the photos with a digital camera. There's posh for ew. He's ordered the camera from the catalogue and then he'll send it back when he's finished with it and tell them it wasn't the right one for him. He's a clever lad. He follows his mam, innit?

Philll can't come to chapel with us today, he's got a patient to see to. There's loads of people back and fore to his surgery, only men as far as I can see. He'll never meet the right woman, mind you, men do suffer mostly don't they with their backs? Look at our Dai's incurable bad back. Our Shantelll said she would help them out if need be, she's dying to be a nurse. Our Philll's been trying that nurses uniform on like. He's such a darling. I'm so glad he's doing well. I knew he'd find a tidy opening and he really does insert himself.

Well, we've had tea and now I'm writing out invites to the wedding. I suppose I'll 'ave to invite that Cherylll, our Gareth's wife. I can't stand her. Miss Cardiff as she is. I'll 'ave to invite that piece next door, Caprice, too. We can make a racket then and she won't complain. I've written the invites on old Xmas cards. I'm telling everyone that we are trying to save the rain forest. People will admire that.

Monday

Three old gents 'ave just knocked on the door. They want to see our Philll. They looked a bit sheepish at me when I opened the door but our Philll soon scuttled them off for treatment. God, he'll 'ave his hands full today. I told him not to bite off more than he can chew. He'll never learn. I told him straight, "All work and no play makes Philllip a dull boy. Make sure you 'ave something nice and warm otherwise you'll come over all funny."

Dai 'ave had a word with his mate that works down the cash and carry and he's going to get a load of pasties and sausage rolls on the knock. That'll save a fortune. He used to be friendly with Shantelll and many a night she popped down to see him after his wife left him for another man. She's such a good talker and listener. I've been to the Co-op and had some Pomagne and flagons of cider. Philll gave me the money from his takings.

Maxine Roxanne is going to be a bridesmaid and Simon, Rapheal and Philllip are going to be page boys. Dai's gonna give her away. Paco's mam and dad, Maria and Manwel, are coming over on Wednesday. Malcolm the taxis is fetching them from sin city airport and there's a rehearsal tomorrow in the chapel. The best man is going to be Rapheal. Philll said he's definitely the best!!!!!

I've got to make a start on cleaning the bedrooms for Maria and Manwel. I've borrowed some bedding from Elsie. We're going to put them in the surgery for the weekend, it'll be nice and warm. We've got a electric convector heater down there and Dai said that we need to use as much electric as possible before the next reading.

Tuesday

We're off down the chapel to practice the walk of shame.

Shantelll wants to 'ave her favrite music played as she walks in: 'Y Viva Espana'. She'll 'ave to try and walk at a tidy pace. It's a jumpy little song mind. She's invited Jamie Owen and Roy Noble to the wedding. I love Roy Noble, I'll 'ave to keep a few pasties back for those two, They'll probably take a load home with them.

The rehearsal went tidy but I'm worried about the dress. Where is she going to get one from? I 'aven't got a clue but as luck would 'ave it, Philll said to me that his old friend Quentin who runs the bridal shop in town will lend our Shantelll a dress for the day and Philll said that he'd fit him in in the surgery next week.

I'm down the surgery at the moment with our Philll and we're preparing the place for Maria and Manwel. Paco's dad will 'ave to make do I'm afraid, as the only mirror we've got is on the ceiling. He'll 'ave to shave laying down. Thank goodness that our Philll 'ave had a shower put in. I'll never know why. I'll put some flowers in as well to make it nice and fresh. There's plenty of tissues and wet wipes here already. Philll's so thoughtful mind.

I think they'll be comfortable enough here. Well, if it's good enough for half the business men in the area, it's good enough for them Spanish people. They 'aven't even got carpets out there.

Tonight I'll 'ave a job on. I'm making confetti out of 20 Argos books, with the paper punch our Shantelll nicked from the solicitor's office last year.

I'm not inviting that Chris Needs. I 'aven't got time to cook separate with Candarels 'cause as you know he's one of them diabolics. I'm sure our Philll is one of them as well, he lives in the toilet.

Wednesday

Them Spanish are arriving today. I hope they don't expect a paella. They'll 'ave stuffed breast of lamb like the rest of us.

There's a knock on the door and there they are: Maria and Manwel, and they've turned up with their youngest son, Rex.

He will 'ave to bunk in with our Elsie next door. I'm sure she'll fit him in.

Our Dai said to Manwel, "'Ow's it going butt?" Manwel asked, "But what?"

We showed them to the surgery and to be honest I think they were quite taken back. The look of shock on their faces, all that carpet on the floor. I'll 'ave to see if we can organise a nice little runner for them to take back with them, our Shantelll knows a fella in the carpet trade. They all sat and had tea with us and the youngest brother is nowhere to be seen. He must be 'aving the time of his life with our Elsie next door.

We puts the telly on to SC4 the Welsh and Maria says, "Oh, I didn't know you could get Norwegian telly here." So I says to her, "It might as well be love."

We've just taken Maria and Manwel up to the club to 'ave a game of bingo. Thank goodness the numbers come up on the screen, they'd never manage otherwise. Dai bought them two Clarks's's's's's pies, you know the ones they make down sin city. Our Dai sucks the inside of the pie out, that's the best way to eat one.

Thursday

We're all getting the nerves now but I'm glad to say that the camera has turned up on a special delivery and Shantelll has gone with Philll down to Quentin's bridal shop to choose a dress that will fit her.

Idwal 'ave soaked his teeth in bleach, they looks like radiators when he does that. Philll and Rapheal are taking Paco out for a stag night somewhere down sin city. They've promised him a night to remember. I hope they don't take him to that funny club where our Dai was singing 'Moon River'.

No sign of Rex. Elsie must be showing him the sights. Mind you, he is 18 and Shantelll told me not to fret. She said, "He's a big boy, he'll come when he's ready."

Shantelll's gone to see her solicitor friend, well I think that's where she's gone. She said something about soliciting. She'd better not be late but she said to me, "Don't worry Mam, I'll be in bed by 9 o'clock."

Dai and me and our Idwal 'ave had an early night. I hope them pasties defrost by the morning.

Friday

Well the big day is here and our Shantelll must 'ave been up early – she's just brought the milk in. She's so thoughtful. The dress is ready. Paco looks dapper in his Matador's outfit. Philll 'ave got his new leather trousers on and Rapheal as well. Idwal stinks of mothballs. I'll 'ave to put a few pineapple chunks in his pockets.

The next thing Elsie and Rex appears, all dressed tidy like and ready for the off. I said to her, "Where 'ave you two been?" Elsie says, "Ooh we 'aven't been anywhere, we've been in the house all the time." She seemed very sheepish mind you.

Shantelll walked down the aisle with Paco to 'Y Viva Espana' and when the minister asked, "Do you take this woman to be your lawful wedded wife?" he said, "Si." Aw, there's romantic for ew. The minister then asked Shantelll, "Do you take this man to be your lawful wedded husband?" She said, "Ay mun."

I think it was all to much for our Elsie. Rex was holding her hand all the way through the service. He seems a nice boy. I think if Elsie had a problem he'd be there like a bull at the gate. I told him he'll 'ave to come again. He's always welcome.

A New Beginning
* WEEK 2 *

HIYA LOVES. IT'S GLADYS here again with the doings that 'ave 'appened here in Ponty Pantin. Well, it was a wild week last week what with Shantelll and Paco's wedding. Anyway here goes...

Saturday

Paco and Shantelll are going on their honeymoon today and she's changing her name by detox. She's now Shantelll Toyah Angharad Conswela Jenkins Rodriges. Tidy mind and they are leaving this afternoon to go to the airport. They are off to Jersey in the Channel Islands, only because she's just realised that her passport has run out. God she's a sledge.

Maria and Manwel are leaving tomorrow. They're going back to Spain. I wonder if they want a bit of carpet to back with? Pity, perhaps they are a bit short, you never know. Rex is adamant that he wants to stay with Elsie, and to be honest they've had a few words. His mam and dad want him to go back with them.

Well, the honeymoon couple are ready for the off and damn they look a picture. Only thing is with our Shantelll, she wears her skirts very short. In fact Dai says to her, "Where are you going with that pelmet?" Off they go and of course I starts to cry but I've got our Cadwalider to keep me going.

Our Philll is doing well with his surgery. Mind you he was going to be a brain surgeon but he soon knocked that on the head.

Later on that evening, me and Dai walks into the club, baby and all. I've put his leather biker's jacket on. Bit nippy now and as soon as we gets through the door the juke box started to play 'Y Viva Espana'. I had to go. It broke my heart. How was my poor Shantelll going to cope with all those foreigners out there in Jersey? She can't even speak the language.

Sunday

No chapel today. I'm too busy seeing to Maria and Manwel. We can't find that Rex anywhere. There was a panic on. We searched everywhere but he was nowhere to be found. Elsie said that he'd gone out for the day and to tell his mam and dad that he was alright and he would contact them when they got back to Spain. It's our Elsie's turn tomorrow to 'ave me in for coffee. She'll tell me all then.

Maria and Manwel left for the airport and they weren't too happy at the thought of leaving Rex behind. I told them straight, "Don't worry, things will sort themselves out. He'll soon be back on his feet." And off they went.

They hadn't gone two minutes when Elsie and Rex appeared and she spilled the beans. They're going out with each other and they want to get married. I was so shocked but they were adamant and they invited me and Dai to 'ave a Chinese meal in town. So off we scoots. Live and let live I say. Anyway, we had this lovely meal but they gave us these stick things to eat the grub. Well, I couldn't get the hang of it, so I calls the nice young waiter over and says quietly in his ear, "I suppose a fork is out of the question?" He soon scarpered. Well, when in Rome, innit?

I looked over the other side of the restaurant and there was a chap looking at a map. I thought, love him, he's lost. Anyway, a little while later he comes over to me and says, "Do you know the way to Merthyr?" So I says, "No love, my husband takes me."

I fancy Elsie is putting on a little bit of weight. Must be contentment. I reckon there's something up there.

Monday

Had no sleep at all. The banging that was going on next door was nobodies business. I mean what a time to put shelves up.

I've just been up the supermarket and I must admit I miss our Shantelll. She always finds the bargains. I must 'ave spent a fortune. On the way back I noticed a lovely young lady going into Philll's surgery. She couldn't 'ave had much wrong with her. She was out in a jiff with a face on her like a smacked assienda.

Damn we had a lovely tea today: brawn and chips. Do you know these Spanish don't know what they're missing. And I've noticed when they make coffee, they use a big massive machine with all steam coming out of it and they bang a lever and you only get a little drop of coffee at the end of it. They'd be better off going down Aldi's.

Dai's brother Willy is off again soon. He's always nipping abroad and bringing things back. Anyway, he's off abroad again. Western Super Mare I think. That's a good run mind and fair play, every time he goes he brings me back duty free fags and 'bacco for Dai. I'm glad that Wales is a separate country now.

Off I went to bed quite down, missing the houseful and the hussell and bustle.

Tuesday

The 'phone goes. It was our Shantelll out in Jersey. She was having a wonderful time. I asks her, "How are you getting on with the language?" She said, "Great Mam. They all speaks English like and the fags are cheap." She said she'd been to the German underground hospital and she said she enjoyed it. Thank goodness for that, I've never liked having internals myself but I'm glad she's alright.

I've got that Jaime Owen on the wireless. He's got lovely blonde hair. I wonder if it's out of a bottle. I can't see any roots when he's on the telly.

We've just had a letter from the Social and they are paying us back two years, some money that we appealed about, so we're having a conservatory put up out the back. I'm not showing the council and Elsie won't say anything. We're having a Jakkusi put in as well. It's for our Dai's incurable bad back. Mind you, we'll 'ave to keep our Idwal out of it. He'll swear he's got bad wind again.

There's a knock on our front door so I opens it and there's our Gareth with Maxine Roxanne. He says to me, "Will you 'ave the little one for a few days Mam? Cherylll's gone shopping."

So here I am with two babies and *Peyton Place* next door. I sits our Maxine Roxanne on my lap and says to her, "Well, what's been going on in your house?" Then she says to me, "Mammy's gone to Western with a man called Willy." I thought, never! Mind you out of some bad comes some good. She can bring back duty free as well as him. I've never liked her but I'll take fags off her on Wednesday.

Gareth's back for the little one and says to me, "Mam, it's all sorted out now, she's back." With that, Willy comes through the door with a face like a hatchet. Later on that day Gareth 'phones me to say that Cherylll, Madam Cardiff, is preggers. I thought to myself, this will be an interesting one – I wonder…

Philll's put a notice in the paper about his surgery. He's taken on Simon now so he's put, 'Buy one get one free'. God, he won't know if he's coming or going.

Went to bingo in the night with Elsie and Rex. I called a line, Elsie called a house and Rex shouted, "Casa!" They make a lovely couple. He was back and fore all night getting her pasties and cornettos. It must be love. I'm glad to see that Elsie has got her appetite back. She used to like a bit of tongue until Dai said to her, "You never know what that cow's been licking." She was never the same after that.

Rex is 'phoning his parents to tell them that he's staying with Elsie and they may even get married. Tomorrow will be an interesting day. If they'd bothered to 'ave a bit of carpet on the floor, none of this would 'ave 'appened.

The manager of the bingo hall, he's posh English, said to me, "Where's your husband?" I said to him, "He's bad," so he says to me, "No he's not, he's welcome here anytime."

A New Beginning
* WEEK 3 *

HIYA LOVES, IT'S GLADYS by 'ere with the 'appenings that 'ave 'appened here in Ponty Pantin.

I'm glad to say that our Shantelll is back from her honeymoon and she seems very happy with her new husband Paco and he loves Cadwalider the baby. Mind you I do wonder who is the father of Cadwalider. Shantelll says she'll know after another 18 tests.

Here goes…

Saturday

Our Dai's gone down to see his old school friend in Tondooo. I think he dabbles a bit in buying and selling. Shantelll 'ave been shopping down the Co-op. Things seem a lot cheaper this week since she's back. She bumped into an old flame, in fact he was her first boyfriend ever. Brian the fisherman. She told me that all these old memories came flooding back. She said, "Oh Mam, he's a lovely boy and a great fisherman and his tackle was famous!!!"

Well the next thing is Xmas and I'm determined to start early this year, so tonight we are all helping to put the decorations up even though there's about 7 or 8 weeks to go. So later on in the evening we gets all the trimmings out of the loft and as per usual the lights wouldn't work, so our Philll replaced one of the bulbs with a red one and we've hung them outside the house.

The tree looked in good nick and none of the tree decorations were broke. Philll was enjoying putting the balls on the branches – he's got flare with trimmings. Idwal told him that he should go on the top of the tree. Idwal seems to think that Philll put the fairy in Briton Ferry, mind you

Philll had him back. They were arguing about the organ in Glamorgan. I didn't know that Id could play a keyboard.

Mind you, the house looks lush and we 'ave had no complaints from the airport so far this year. It looks like Blackpool illusinations.

Sunday

Dai 'ave left a load of boxes in the hallway and when I went into the parlour, well I couldn't move. Boxes everywhere. I hope nobody calls from the Customs and Exercise.

Anyway, Idwal's old friend 'ave died under strange circumfrances. Apparently he was making love to his wife at the time and she's a strange piece to be honest, because when the funeral was going down the street she wouldn't 'ave the lid of the coffin on. She left it off and as the parade was going through our street me and our Elsie popped out the front to see him off like and Elsie said, "Well I don't believe it. Oh pity, only one tulip."

I think our Shantelll has got something to tell me and Dai. She wants to see us later on after tea. She's got something to say. Anyway, she sits us down later on that evening and she spilled the beans, she's preggers again but she's ever so worried. "What if it can't speak English, Mam?" she asked. I told her, "Don't worry. Paco will translate for us."

Later on that night there was a bit on the news about stolen goods. Our Dai turned it over straight away. He doesn't like things like that, he's such a good man.

Went to bed early that night, I'm cleaning up the club in the morning.

Monday

I was up at the crack of dawn, done a bit of tidying up and off I goes to the club. After I shoved all them pineapple chunks in the urinals, our Dai and Paco turned up with the boxes. They sounded like glass. I think he must 'ave had some ashtrays on the cheap for the steward. He's got a heart of gold.

Dai went down the airport to meet his cousin Len. I asked

our Dai, "Do you think you will recognise him?" Dai said, "No he's been away for donkey's years. But he should recognise me. I 'aven't been anywhere."

I always remember when our Idwal was working. He used to work with the sewerage for the council and I never forget, it was a warm day and he took off his jacket and it slipped into the manhole full of poo poo. Our Idwal went to retrieve the jacket and his mate told him, "Don't bother, the jacket will be ruined." Idwal told him straight, "I'm not worried about the jacket, I can get another one off the council. But my sandwiches and fags are in the pocket."

Tuesday

Shantelll went to sin city on the train and had a day out shopping with the girls and she got blotto. On the way back in the train she was sat opposite a minister and he said to her, "Don't speak to me girl, you're drunk." So she says to him, "Look at you, you must 'ave had a few, you've put your collar on back to front." Anyway, she managed to get home and went straight to bed to sleep it off.

Later on that night there was a knock on the door, so I peeps through the curtains and there were two official men with brief cases outside. I said to our Dai, "We'll 'ave to get them boxes out into Elsie's next door." So Dai and Id and Elsie moved them one by one around the back into Elsie's front room and I was shouting, "I won't be a minute. I'm in the shower and I'm drying my hair. I won't be long." So then I sticks my head under the tap and grabbed a towel. Dai, Id and Elsie were knackerated. So I opens the door and says, "Sorry about that," drying my hair. "What can I do for you?" Do you know what they said? "Would you like a copy of the Witch Tower?" I mean to say. After all that juggling about. It's a pity that our Shantelll wasn't about. She gets rid of them sharpish like. She normally opens the door in her bask and blows them a kiss. They don't hang around then.

We had a beautiful tea in the evening: chips and pickle vinegar. Lush.

Wednesday

It's our Philll's birthday today and we've organised a surprise party up the club for tonight. He doesn't know a thing about it 'cause he've been so busy seeing to all them bad backs down his surgery. We've got a fab buffet for him: cheese on sticks and paste sandwiches. I've cut up 14 sliced loaves altogether but the big surprise is a giant cake that's hollow and we've got a girl to jump out of the cake in a bikini. He'll love it.

The trouble I've had trying to keep this a secret you'd never believe. Our Idwal keeps saying, "I hope there won't be loads of pansies up the club tonight," and I keep telling him, "It's nothing to do with horticulture love," but that will put Philll off the scent.

Anyway, the moment of truth came and our Philll walked into the club right on time and he was totally overwhelmed and started to cry. All his friends were there: Jason from the Dream Lads, Quentin from the bridal shop, a boy with plucked eyebrows called Popsie and loads of men in leather outfits, damn they looked smart and to be honest, I've never seen women with Adam's apples before but there was a few there.

So later on that night we all sang 'Happy Birthday' to Philll and the girl jumped out of the cake and asked Philll, "Would you like supersex?" and our Philll, good boy as he is, said to her, "I'll just 'ave the soup love." Aww, too embarrassed to kiss her in front of me. Love him.

Thursday

The Social's coming round today to give us a means test. We used to take all of the stuff out of the house and put it in Elsie's, then I'd put up the old curtains with holes in them. But we've decided it's too much work, so what we do now is swap the front door numbers with Elsie and she sits in ours in perfect splendour and we goes in hers until the Social 'ave done their business.

Anyway, in they came and took one look at the house and said straight away, "I think we'll 'ave to give you a decorating grant Mrs Jenkins and an increase on your book." So I says, "Thank you kind sir. Isn't Wales a wonderful country that we live in? I wouldn't live anywhere else. Maybe now we can afford some lamb chops. Oh Xmas will be wonderful this year for us. Thank you sir!!!!!!"

I closed the door and as soon as they went I thought what a pillack and went back into ours. Elsie asks, "Did you get any more money?" So I told her no, the house was adequate, but I will give her a carton of fags for her trouble. There's plenty in the parlour.

Friday

I'm going with our Dai to town to get some new shoes and he's got to call to the doctor about his incurable bad back. So off we goes to the shoe shop and he must 'ave tried on two dozen pairs of shoes. He kept on saying, "They're too tight," so the man in the shop said to try them with the tongue out. So Dai said with his tongue stuck out, "They're still too tight."

Anyway, we gets to the doctors and in he went and the doctor said to him, "Go to the window and stick your tongue out." So he did for about five minutes and then he said to the doctor, "Why am I sticking my tongue out by here?" and the doctor said, "I can't stand that woman opposite."

Shantelll's got a phrase book to learn Spanish for when the new baby do come look, 'cause Paco's the father like, but she's adamant that she'll crack the language. Like she said the other day, "Spanish must be easy, there's two year olds speaking it out in Spain."

A New Beginning
* WEEK 4 *

HIYA LOVES, IT'S GLADYS here again with the 'appenings that 'ave 'appened here in Ponty Pantin.

Well what a week it was last week, what with Philll's birthday and of course the Social coming around. But we showed them: life's for living not working day and night. Anyway, here goes…

Saturday

As you know, we've got a brand new car on the mobility, but we've still got the old banger out the back lane and Dai's dying to get rid of it. So his mate up the club said to him, "Dai, why don't you take the car down my garage and I'll turn the clock back for you?" So Dai nipped the car down there and indeed he turned the clock back shedfulls.

Later on that day I said to our Dai, "'aven't you put that car of yours in the paper yet?" Dai says, "No I 'aven't bothered, after all, it's only done 28,000 miles."

Our Shantelll went for a walk with Paco down the fields and she walked across a bridge. As Paco was about to follow her, the bridge collapsed and Shantelll was stranded on the other side. She said to him, "You'll 'ave to get help," but Paco replied, "No, wait until it's dark and I'll shine my torch and you can cross on the beam." God he's so thick, but our Shantelll was one up on him. She said, "No way, hose. I'll start to cross and you'll turn off the beam and I'll fall in. You must think I'm stupid."

Anyway, on the way back Paco said, "Look Shantelll, there's a dead bird." But she couldn't see it anywhere. When she got home she told me about the dead bird incident. She said, "Mam, I couldn't see it at all. I looked up everywhere!"

She's as dull as a brush.

We're going on a pleasure cruise tomorrow on a boat over to Western. We can't wait. Philll is so excited – he just loves Fisherman's Friends. I told him to make sure he's got some to suck on, on the way over.

Sunday

Bedlam as per usual. There's me cutting sandwiches, Dai's packing Woodbines in his duffle bag and Shantelll must think she's going on an ocean liner. She's taken the skimpiest skirts that she could find. Idwal's wearing his medals in case someone thinks he's the captain and poor Maxine Roxanne is spewing everywhere and she 'aven't left dry ground yet. Philll's got his rubber air bed with him just in case. I told him, "Why bother taking that air bed with you? You'll be blowing all day." Silly boy. He should be looking for a tidy girl.

Anyway, on we goes on this ship thing and it starts to move off towards Western. We've all got our passports with us, 'cause as you know Wales is run different to England now. I'm a little worried because Paco didn't apply for a visa. Never mind, the English are half tidy people ain't they?

While we was on the ship there was a seaman giving our Shantelll the eye all the time, he never let up at all. I told her, "If he carries on like that, I'll 'ave to lock your port hole tonight." But I must admit, it was a lovely change. The only thing was that the fags were the same price as Wales. Whatever 'appened to duty free?

Monday

Glad to be home. Maxine Roxanne was as good as gold. She only spewed three times in the dining room. Love her. And what do you think? Elsie's filling in a form to be an auxiliary nurse. Anyway, she filled it in and she brought it in to me to check it over. It said 'Fill in the meanings of these medical terms', so these are her answers:

Artery – the study of painting; Bacteria – back door of

the cafeteria; Bowels – aeiou; Caesarean section – an area of Rome; Coma – a punctuation mark; D and C – where Washington is; Dilate – to live long; Impotent – distinguished and well known; Fibula – a small lie; Labour pain – to get hurt in work; Nitrate – cheaper than day rate; Pelvis – cousin of Elvis; Recovery room – place to do upholstery; Seizure – a Roman emperor; Terminal illness – sick in the airport; Tibia – a country in North Africa; Urine – opposite of your out; Vein – conceited.

I don't think somehow she's going to get it, she'd better go back to the Co-op.

I must tell you that Elsie was out driving the other day showing that Rex around the town and she went down a one-way street. The police stopped her and said, "Where are you going?" She said, "I don't know love, but it can't be very good there, all the other cars are leaving."

Tuesday

I just been out the front to check the post in the new cast iron mailbox we've had, then I goes back in the house. Five minutes later I went back to check the mail box again and went back in the house. I did this about six times to be honest and then nosey next door, Caprice asked, "Why are you back and fore to the mailbox?" So I told her straight, "I'm trying to master this new computer we've got. It keeps telling me, 'You've got mail'." Do you know she's as thick as two short planks.

Philll's doing well with his surgery – he's taking a fortune, and all cash. I told him it's best to 'ave it in the hand, you won't 'ave to show nothing then.

The new Jakkusi 'ave come. It's a portable one, so we're putting it in Philll's surgery for the time being but I'm a bit annoyed with Philll, he must be washing his hair in it. You can see the conditioner in the water, naughty boy. But it's right handy if you've got a ton of washing – it's like an old twin tub. Brilliant.

Our Philll's buying a new sports car as he's doing so well,

you know the sort: one with a lid coming on Friday. I can't wait to see that.

Wednesday

As you know, we've screwed the Social yet again and we're all going to 'ave another 'oliday out of the painting grant. The trouble is where should we go? I loves Benidorm. Shantelll wants to go to Turkey, she fancies some Turkish Delight. I told her she should get a box full up Makkros. Philll fancies Sydney, Dai's quite happy as long as there's a bookies handy. We'll see where we end up before long I suppose.

We settled down to listen to Radio Wales. Philll loves Chris Needs and Jamie Owen, they're his favrites. We all want to join Chris's's's's's Garden. I want to be called Gladys Gardeenier, Dai wants to be Dai the Dude, Idwal is happy enough to be called the old count. Shantelll doesn't care what she's called as per usual and Philll and Rapheal want to be called the Prickly Pansies.

Idwal came into the living room with a face like thunder. I said, "What's the matter Id?" He said, "What's the time now?" I said, "10 to 11 love," and Id said, "Do you know, I've asked that question four times today and every time someone gives me a different answer."

Shantelll's beginning to show a little. I'm so glad for the two of them. They're a lovely couple and she's still learning Spanish. She can say sangria, San Migwel and si.

Foreign Parts
* WEEK 1 *

HIYA LOVES, GLADYS HERE with the 'appenings that 'ave 'appened in our lovely Ponty Pantin.

We just got back from seeing Rapheal and Paco's family in Spain. Nice place but a poor country: no carpets, no coal fires and no central heating. God love 'em.

Anyway you know what they're all like around here for pressies. I had another stuffed donkey for Elsie next door. It had saddle bags on it as well. Our Dai said they'd be handy to keep fags in on the way 'ome. He doesn't like to show how much he smokes! I bought our Gareth a bottle of Bacardi. God knows he needs a drink having to cope with that wife of his, and I got four Spanish dolls for his Maxine Roxanne. I didn't tell our Dai 'cause he'd have had fags up those dresses as well.

I saw our Philll talking to two Spanish blokies on our last day there. Well, I saw him chatting to loads of Spanish fellas throughout the week but this pair at the airport, I'm sure they were after a couriers job over here. He's made such an impression on them. The Spaniards were kissing him on both cheeks. Well they do that out there don't they? I am sure he's bi-lingual but he won't talk to us about it. I make do with hand gestures.

Our Shantelll 'ave bought a Spanish flamingo dress. She wants to wear it up the club. Damn, she'll turn some heads! Mind you, at the airport she had a right face on her. I said to her, "What's the matter our Shantelll?" She says to me look, "I wanted to visit the Basque region." I says to her, "'aven't you got enough knickers? You've got tons of lingerie."

When we gets on the plane our Idwal was so disappointed there were no flying waitresses, only flying waiters. Lovely eyebrows they had an' all. One of them kept on talking to our Philll and giving him Champain – loads of it and they kept going back and fore to the toilet. In there ages they were, but eventually they come out of there with a smile on our Philll's face. I told him all this fancy licquor is no good to him. He's better having it all up.

Saturday

I've got to shift myself today, loads of washing and I've got to nip around and take these pressies to the clan. Elsie loved her stuffed donkey, she's got two now in the toilet. She's landed.

Our Philll 'ave had a new set of nail varnish, he wants to be like Robbie Williams and Beckham. Damn, it suits him tidy and he've got his hair in a ponytail as well, he's such a glamorous little thing.

Our Giro has come this morning, I'll 'ave to try and claim some more now, knowing that them Spanish are coming over to stay again soon. Dai told Manwel that he goes to the pool every Tuesday night, so they're all bringing their bathers. Strange people.

Shantelll is out again with her collecting tins. I don't know why she bothers, she filled six tins the other week and there was only £2.38 in the whole lot.

Rapheal 'ave had a lovely new car, his mam and dad 'ave given him the money for it. While he was out up the estate in it he had a punchure, so out he gets to mend the wheel and while he was getting the wheel off, a lad jumped in the car and said to our Rapheal, "If you're having the wheels, I'm having the radio."

We're not going to the club tonight because our Dai 'ave brought back a load of San Migwel from Spain. Lush it is.

Philll is off to the hospital for a check up on Monday. I hope he'll be alright. He could 'ave gone sooner but he was waiting for this new Italian man doctor, so he's seeing him Monday, fair play. If he'd seen that lovely young lady doctor he would 'ave been head over heels with her.

Sunday

The baby's being taken to chapel today for the first time and we're all going as well. Damn he looks lush in his new fluffy booties, napkin and biker's jacket. So anyway, we all goes like: me, Dai, Id, the boys, Shantelll and the nipper. As soon as I gets in to the chapel I says my little prayer as I always do and then realises that there is two collections and I only had a 2p piece. Shantelll says, "Don't worry Mam, I'll nip outside with my collecting tin. I'll sort it."

No sooner had the minister started his sermon than the baby filled his napkin. 'umming he was. Mrs Williams from up the road had to go, she said she'd left the meat on and she didn't want it to burn. I thought to myself, it must be warm in here, everyone's using their mini fans. What a waste of 'lectric, no wonder they've got two collections.

We had a lovely tea that evening: bread and dripping. Our Philll loves the brown bit at the bottom, he can't get enough of it. I've got our Philll's clean underclothes ready for tomorrow, well I can't 'ave people talking about us can I?

Monday

Dai's gone to work in his dark glasses, you never know who's about do you? I'm getting on with the washing, don't talk to me about nappies. I told our Philll that Terries are the best. Philll quite agreed.

Anyway, Philll's gone to the hospital, he 'ave had the chance to go to college to become a male nurse. He said he couldn't wait to enter.

Dai's brother Willy is back from Bangcok and he've brought some lovely things back for us. I've had a lovely Bancockian night shirt (I think they call them a commode), 'bacco for our Dai, sweets for our Idwal and lovely earrings for our Shantelll. He wouldn't show me what he'd brought back for our Philll. I didn't 'ave a clue, but it was in a long box. It must 'ave been a salami or something.

Anyway, Philll's back from the hospital and he seems quite happy. Things must 'ave gone well, he's got such a smile on his face. I say to him, "How did it go love?" He said to me, "That lovely male Italian doctor was very good, he checked me over everywhere." So I asked him, "Did he check you down by there with the glove and gel?" and our Philll says to me, "Yes Mam. I told him to do it again as I wanted a second opinion." Well you can't be to sure nowerdays, can you?

I told our Philll that Willy's been to Bangcok, Philll said, "Oh I hope not!!!!!"

Tuesday

Elsie's in as per usual for her morning coffee. I gets the cheap one from town for her – she can't tell the difference anyway – and we've got Jamie Owen on the wireless. Damn he's got a lovely little voice. I 'ave written to him to see if our Philll could 'ave a tour of his studio, you never know, our Philll might get in there one day, and I love that Nicola Wayward whatsaname. She's lush. If she ever wanted a 'oliday our Shantelll said she would sit in for her and take her tin with her at the same time.

Idwal is off with the old age on a trip. They're off to somewhere down sin city to play bingo for the day. That should keep him out of mischief for a while, but on the way down the bus conked out and they all had to wait for a replacement, so they all gets out for a walk in the trees. Idwal says to his mate Mansell, "Look at that ladybird on the front of that tree." So Mansell says to him, "How do you know if that's the front of the tree?" So our Idwal says to him someone's just done their business round the back. Anyway, the bus arrives and they eventually gets to the bingo. Our Idwal won £50 and gave me a tenner. Our Philll said he had a tenner last week.

There's a good film on the telly box tonight so we're all staying in with a take away: chicken coorma, onion bajis and a ton of those big crisps. Can't wait.

Wednesday

Our Shantelll was very disappointed: she rented a film from the video shop today and when she got it home all she could see was white lines on the screen. So she took it back and said to the blokie behind the counter, "There's something wrong with this film." So he told her to choose another one. She said she'd never been so disappointed. I said to her, "What was the film called?" She said, *"Head Cleaner."* So I told her I'd try and get it for her in town look.

Our Shantelll has had another two designer dresses. I don't know where the money is coming from, but damn she looks smart.

Thursday

Pay day today and I'm glad to be honest, because the Giro don't last long does it? I'm trying to put a bit aside every week so that I can show off a bit in front of Rapheal's parents, Maria and Manwel. I've got it all planned: bingo Monday, bingo Tuesday, bingo Wednesday, club on Thursday, party and buffet on Friday, down the dog track on Saturday and chapel on Sunday. They'll enjoy that I'm sure.

We 'aven't got a bidet so they'll 'ave to wash their smalls in the washing machine like everyone else.

Idwal said that he'd get some fresh chickling in instead of the frozen, they'll love it.

Foreign Parts
* WEEK 2 *

HIYA LOVES, IT'S GLADYS here again with the 'appenings that 'ave 'appened here in Ponty Pantin.

I've got a bit of shopping to do for Xmas and our Dai's brother Willy is getting a few things for me on the knock. Can't wait. Well you've got to look after number one 'aven't you? If the weather won't kill you, that lot at the end of the M4 in London will.

Saturday

Our Philll 'ave had a bit of trouble with the roof of his surgery. It's leaking and he 'ave tried to mend it himself to save a bit of money. But it's no good. He 'ave had a man in for the day to block the hole. I told him it'll cost him dearly and Merthyr wasn't built in a day. It's a bit of a job. It'll be long and hard, but it'll be worth it in the end.

I want our Cadwalider to start going to chapel regular like. It's important for him to learn the 10 amendments. It 'aven't done me any harm.

Mind you, there's a new woman moved in to Ponty Pantin on her own and she wears strange clothes: Doctor Martens and jeans, and her head is shaved at the sides. Mind you, they tell me she's very clean, she has a woman in three times a week, aw love her. Apparently, she had a husband once but he ran away with her best friend Jean and they say she misses her like mad.

Dai 'ave gone down to hemorrhoid city, Pyle that is. He's meeting his Willy down there, picking a few things up I suppose.

While I was out earlier with our Cadwalider and Shantelll having burger and chips, two Americans stopped me and asked me how to pronounce the place we was in. They didn't 'ave a clue about the Welsh language, so Shantelll told them, "BURRRRRGERRRR KING."

Sunday

Me and Dai are laying in bed like and I feels something touching my leg. I thought, don't start now good boy, I'm not in the mood for all this. But I could still feel something touching my leg so I turns to our Dai and says, "Oi you, sling yer hook." But Dai was asleep so I looks under the bed clothes and lo and behold it was a ferret cwtching in to me! Apparently, Dai got it off his Willy without telling me. Mind you the little might looked half starved. So I calls out, "Shantelll!" and tells her, "Get something for this little git will you?" So she takes the ferret downstairs and makes him corned beef and chips. Aw, he devoured it. Dai was chuffed to 'ave a ferret but I warned him, if it pees on my catalogue again, he'll be in the dog house.

Mind you our Shantelll had our Idwal going the other day. She said to him, "Id, guess what's in my bag. It's long, it runs on batteries, it vibrates and it's about eight inches long when extended." Aw she had him in a tizz, then she pulled out her mobile phone. She's a girl and a half.

Dai's favrite tonight: brawn sandwiches, but our Philll is into Rudyard Kiplin, he reckons he makes exceedingly good cakes.

Monday

Our Shantelll is setting the video tonight to watch something called *Pussy Galore*. I suppose it's all about that Rolf Harris operating on cats all night. I can't handle that.

Our Idwal 'ave just come back from the pet shop and apparently he asked the man inside for a wasp and the man told him, "We don't sell them." But our Idwal put him straight. He said, "What are you talking about? You had one in the window yesterday." These people should really do a bit of stock taking.

Mind you I remember our Philll when he was a little boy

and he had a tortoise and he said to me, "Mam, what'll 'appen when my tortoise dies?" So I told him, "Aw love, we'll 'ave a funeral and lots of sandwiches and cakes and singing." He said to me, "Aw Mam, can I kill it now?"

Mind you he works awful hard. I can hear those poor men moaning like hell down his surgery. They must 'ave awful bad backs.

Two brothers down the road 'ave won the lottery. Two million each and they went to London for a bit of a break. Cledwyn and Mansell. Lovely boys. Anyway Cled went in to a chip shop and bought pie and chips each. Lush. Then as they were going down the road they fancied a sports car each, so Cled said, "I'll get these," but Mansell said, "No I'll get these, you got the pies."

Tuesday

The ferret is settling in tidy and we always give him his favrite food: corn flakes and ice cream in the morning and at tea time he has a bit of cod from the chippy. I've got to give him the best. Dai loves him as if he were his own. Mind you, the dog Christine dragged the ferret though the house earlier on. He though it was one of my fluffy slippers. Silly pooch.

Me and our Elsie next door are thinking of starting up a catering service, sandwiches in a van and going all around the place. We've got the name already: 'Ponty Pantin Pastries'.

Anyway, we've got our eye on a van. It used to belong to a farmer, he used to carry hazardous waste in it but that's not a problem, nothing a bit of elbow grease and a few pineapple chunks from up the club wouldn't put right.

We works out a menu on the computer: sandwiches consist of spam and Brawn paste and then we've got French rolls, one called the 'Gobblin Special', a turkey torpedo roll.

Shantelll gets the food from the Co-op, somehow she gets it cheaper there than the cash and carry. She's a clever girl. Anyway, we goes to see the van down the road with the farmer and to be honest it's not too bad. Philll's friend Claudius is going to put the name on the van for us. So we bought the van and were very excited. Philll went up and drove it over to 'ave it painted.

Wednesday

Philll came back and showed us the van and Claudius had put on it: 'Ponty Pantin Pastries – You name it, we'll fill it!' Aw he's awful artistic.

There was all hell on getting the food together. We had sausage rolls, pasties that Elsie had made and dog biscuits for Christine, 'cause he's travelling with us in the back just in case we meet some ruffians. Philll and Shantelll 'ave phoned up a load of offices and businesses to tell them about this new service, so we were just about ready for the off: pinnies ready, white hats and left over rubber gloves from Philll's surgery. I'm not wasting anything let me tell you, and we had to be at our first port of call at about 11.30.

So we loads up the van, Duw it smelt lovely and we sat in ready for the off. Then we realised that me and Elsie couldn't drive. We'd forgotten about that but thank God, our Shantelll's Paco came to the rescue. The only thing is he tends to drive on the wrong side of the road.

We eventually got around the lot of them and it seemed to go real well. There was only one complaint: a woman said she found a hair in her egg mayonnaise. But Paco came to the rescue again with his Spanish accent. He told her it was a Spanish boocaroni, not a dog's hair. Then she swallowed the rest of it and ordered more for the next day.

Foreign Parts
* WEEK 3 *

WELL HIYA LOVES, IT'S Gladys here with the 'appenings that 'ave 'appened here again in wonderful Ponty Pantin and I've got tumps to do.

I still can't find that blue film for our Philll, that's his favrite group, Blue. Shantelll and Paco seem to be doing fine but I think he's missing Spain a bit. He wants our Shantelll and the baby Cadwalider to move out there. I mean to say, a third world country with no carpets. I can't see that 'appening. Anyway, here goes...

Saturday

Philll is starting photography and he needs a dark room to develop the pictures, so I'm keeping all the old light bulbs that 'ave gone, that should keep the room nice and dark for him. He's so artistic, Mammy's little soldier. And by all accounts he's got some male models coming this afternoon to pose for him. I think they are modelling special corsets for their bad backs. Mind you, Philll always says by the time he's 30 he wants three animals in his life: a mink on his back, a jaguar in the garage and a tiger in his bed. Oh, he's a boy mind.

Idwal is getting on fine with the wine making but there's a hell of a smell upstairs, must be the ingredients. Talking of which, I'm meant to be on diet at the moment but I'm not staying on it no more for a number of reasons: fattening food is cheaper, it's coming up to winter and I needs a bit of fat on me – that'll save on gas – and I won't lose a lot of weight anyway. I've got heavy bones.

There's a lovely night up the club tonight. Philll's organised it. It's like a happy hour but he's done it in a different way. He's called it 'gay time'. He's pinched that idea from *The*

Flintstones: 'We'll 'ave a gay old time'.

Dai said he wouldn't go because he doesn't fancy his chances on the bingo. Mind you, he should go, he generally wins. I bet he'd pick up something there, it's nice to 'ave a bob in your hand.

Sunday

The house is so quiet. They're all still in bed, mind you, Philll didn't finish until 4 this morning. He saw lots of old friends there last night. They were all hugging and kissing him.

Mind you, our Dai is easy to please – he's got simple needs. He can survive the weekend with only three things: beer, boxer shorts and batteries for the remote.

Idwal has presented me with the first bottle of wine. It's called 'Idwal's Liquour' and we're having it with our Sunday dinner today, if they ever surface that is.

Shantelll went down to the chemist to get some deodourant for her bottom and she asked the woman behind the counter for some but the woman said to our Shantelll, "We don't sell deodorant for the bottom." Shantelll argued with her for ages but it was no good.

So Shantelll scooted off home, ran in the house and picked up her nearly used deodourant up and scooted off back to the chemist. Then she showed it to her and the woman said, "But this is ordinary roll on deodorant." So Shantelll says back to her, "Look, it says clearly on the side: 'To use, push up bottom.' "

Monday

Came home from shopping and I bought some hot cross buns. When Dai saw them he said, "Well done Gladys, you've baked buns with my signature on them."

Mind you, Cled down the road borrowed the steam roller to nip and see his brother in the next village but he was awful unlucky. He was done for three bald tyres. Aw love him.

Philll has got quite a few blokes going back and fore to his surgery. He must be hell bent on making a go of things.

All the people that 'ave been to him 'ave all said that they 'ave been touched by his loyalty.

The sandwich round 'ave died a death. The van we bought has got a lot of things wrong with it, in fact our Idwal went out in it for a spin after he'd been to the club and the police stopped him and said, "Idwal you are drunk." And our Idwal said, "Thank God for that, I thought the steering had gone for a Burton now." Thank God they didn't press charges and they sent their very best wishes to our Shantelll.

I've been telling our Dai to go to the local gym, but it is hard for him, especially if you want to be as fit as a fiddle and you're shaped like a cello. I told our Dai to take up jogging – at least I'd 'ave some heavy breathing again.

I think it's important to stay in shape. My grandmother used to walk five miles a day and after three weeks we never knew where she got to. But there you are, I tells our Dai not to worry about middle age. He'll grow out of it.

Tuesday

Elsie's in for her usual coffee, always when that Jamie Owen is on the wireless, and we were talking about her last birthday party. Oh damn it was good. The only thing that Elsie didn't like was the cake. There were that many candles on it, she was driven back by the flames. Mind you, she's getting on well with Paco's younger brother, Rex. He treats her like royalty but she told me that he wants sex all the time, even at the traffic lights the other day. But like she says, she only wants a bit of nonsense when they install a new pope. I can't see that relationship lasting too long.

I've got to tell you that our local vicar has been having an affair with one of his church ladies and apparently they were seen romping in the grass by one of the other church goers. Well, would you believe it? Anyway, apparently this church goer said to our vicar, "Do you need a car?" and the vicar said, "No not really." Anyway, to cut a long story short, the vicar bought the car from the church goer to keep him quiet about his doings with the lady. It was an old banger and he paid

£1,500 for it. Later on, the vicar tried to start the old car and it wouldn't start, so our Shantelll said to him, "How much did you pay for that old banger?" The vicar said "£1,500," and our Shantelll told him straight, "Someone saw you coming, good boy!"

Wednesday

Our Shantelll is trying to keep fit and she goes to the gym twice a week. I don't know where she gets the energy from now she's a part-time nurse with our Philll in the surgery. God that girl has got her hands full.

So, as I was saying, our Shantelll goes to the gym twice a week and she met Blod from down the road there while she was changing. Our Shantelll noticed that Blod was putting on men's underpants, so our Shantelll asked her, "Why are you wearing men's underpants?" Blod told her it was ever since the boyfriend found them in her car. I don't understand that!!!

Mind you, that boy down the road, Cled, he's as thick as two short planks. He used to work on a farm and I remember his mother telling me all about him and his job. He apparently told the farmer, "Hold these two sheep down while I count them." Anyway, he apparently met a girl in a bar in sin city and he chatted her up and asked her did she want a lift home. But she said to him, "I can't tonight love, I 'ave my menstrual cycle," and Cled said, "Don't worry about that love, we can put it in the back of my van."

Thursday

Do you know, our Dai has no work in him really, and if it wasn't for me keeping it all together, this house would be in shambles. I must admit, Dai 'ave converted me to religion. I never believed in hell till I married him, but he's alright really. Mind you he said to me this morning, "I don't know why you wear a bra, you've got nothing to put in it." So I told him straight, "You wear pants don't you?"

Philll has got a full day today, they're coming from everywhere and he won't know which way to turn the way he's going. But the money is rolling in, so I don't mind. Well it keeps him off the streets don't it.

Rex is a nice boy. He treats Elsie well, but I can't help but worry, it's like putting Sterling Moss in a Ford Anglia. I hope it works out for them.

I do believe that the Spaniards are coming over again soon to try and bring him back with them, we'll see what 'appens there.

There's a programme on telly tonight called *Twin Peaks*. Our Dai thinks it's about Dolly Parton.

Friday

Pay day today. Willy still gives me £100 a week and I don't even see him that much. He's out all the time wealing and dealing. He gave me a lovely facial sauna the other day, and all was well until Idwal started steaming veg in it. I'll be glad when Id goes up the centre and gives me a break.

Anyway, I want our Cadwalider to speak the three spokes: Welsh, English and Spanish. It's important to 'ave a bit of Welsh these days, I'm all for it. I went to town and outside the market there was the fisherman and he was shouting, "Fresh fish, fresh fish!" So I goes up to him and says, "Why don't you say it in Welsh?" So he shouts, "Fish fresh, fish fresh!" Oh it's nice to be fluent mind.

While I was out I saw our Philll in a ladies booteek buying fishnet tights. They must be a present for our Shantelll. He always insists on good quality, well he's got the money now hasn't he? He's so fussy, he was even trying them on. He's such a darling.

Simon is still working for him. Philll's very good with him as well as paying him well. He gives it to him in the hand, can't beat it can you love?

Foreign Parts
* WEEK 4 *

WELL WHAT A WEEK – the Xmas shopping is doing my Ponty Pantin head in. But as per usual, I'll cope. I always do. Anyway, here goes with the doings that 'ave 'appened...

Saturday

Our Elsie next door is as dull as a brush. She went to a compartment store in sin city and this flussy piece with loads of make up on came up to her and said that toilet water was the best for Elsie's completion. So Elsie goes home determined to look younger and to use only toilet water on her face. She is such a sledge, she came in by here and told me that she wouldn't be using toilet water again – the seat kept falling on her head.

Mind you, our Philll is into everything going. He was only saying the other day about keeping crevices clean and I agreed with him. You never know what gets into crevices these days.

We are all on that new margarine now, you know the one, it's called Flora Automatic, lovely mind!!!

Our Idwal is trying to get on *Pop Idol* on the tellybox, he's having his hair spiked and singing a Moira Anderson medley. His favrite tune is 'On the Banks of the Warbash' and he's borrowing our Philll's ripped jeans as well. Well, you can't keep a good man down, that's what I do say!!!

We're ordering a take away for tonight. We're having chicken coorma and rice and chips and to be honest, you 'ave to watch every penny these days don't you? I've got some chicken portions in the freezer so I'll cook them quick like and I've got packet rice and microwave chips, so that all I'm ordering is a curry sauce. That'll do tidy. They'll never know the difference.

Sunday

Dai went down the club. There was an open day for people to try and get new jobs and to get advice on things like. What exactly I don't know, but off him and his mate Maldwin went, to see what was what.

When they got there they were giving away new clothes if you weren't working, so our Dai and Maldwin ques up and when it was their turn, this blokie asked their sizes. Dai wasn't sure because I buy all his clothes. So Maldwin said to Dai, "You look a bit bigger than me, just add one size on to everything I say, that should do you tidy."

So Maldwin was asked what size shoes and Maldwin said, "Eights," so Dai said, "Nines." Then the blokie asked Maldwin what size chest and Maldwin said, "46," so Dai says, "47 like." Then the blokie asked Maldwin what size hat and Maldwin said, "Six and seven eighths," so Dai said, "Nine ten." Mind you he was lucky, the clobber fitted Dai tidy.

Monday

Caprice is trying to sell her house and there's a board outside saying 'For Sale'. Anyway, I was in her house the other day and there was a knock on the door, and there was the estate agent with some people to look around the house. So she let's them in and starts to give them the tour. I puts my shillings worth in, mind, saying that the neighbours are fabs. Anyway, Caprice had a 'phone call and asked me to hold the fort. So I says to the prospective buyers, "Well this is a lovely little area. To the north you 'ave the chemical works and to the south you 'ave the slaughter house, and that's a great advantage." "Oh?" says the woman. "How's that then?" I says back to her, "You know which way the wind is coming from." They never bought the house. Strange.

I went to town and saw Shantelll and we had a chat and I told her that I wanted a pair of new boots, and Shantelll said to me, "Look Mam, I've just bought a pair of new boots myself." So I says, "Where did you get them from?" and Shantelll said to me, "From that shop in the centre." I says, "Which one?" and she says back to me, "Both of them."

Tuesday

I was reading the newspaper the other morning and I read that people that are over weight, it could be caused by a virus. So anyway our Dai comes in puffing and pantin' – knackerated he was. So he says to me, "Anything good in the paper today?" So I tells him about overweight and the virus and furthermore I said, "If you don't feel well tomorrow, why don't you 'phone in fat?"

Our Idwal was tootieing down and was face to face with the dog and he was saying, "Meow, meow," in the dog's face. I said, "Why are you doing that our Id?" So he says back to me, "It's good for the dog to 'ave a second language."

I had a strange dream the other night. I dreamed that Dai had bought me this really expensive gold necklace, real expensive it was. So I asked our Dai what the dream meant and he said in my ear, "Wait until tonight." Anyway, I waited all day and in comes our Dai with a present for me. So I opens it and there it was: a book called *The Meaning of Dreams*. Mind you, he bought a lovely thermometer for the wall, but I said to him, "Dai, you should 'ave waited 'till the summer, you'd 'ave got more mercury for your money."

Wednesday

Shantelll 'ave had a job down the factory, making dolls. Pretty things they are as well. They're called 'Tickle Me' dolls but there was a bit of a hold up in the production line. Shantelll was sewing seecwin marbles on to the doll and the manager told her straight, "Shantelll, what I said was, 'Give each doll two test tickles'." She didn't last there long, love her!

That reminds me of when our Shantelll was in a swimming competition in school years ago. They had to do five lengths of the pool doing the breast stroke and our Shantelll came in last, about 20 minutes behind. So the lifeguard said to her, "Why are you so slow Shantelll?" And she told him straight, "It's not fair, you told us it was the breast stroke and all them other girls cheated. They were using their arms."

Dai came in drunk the other night with his mate Maldwin. They could hardly stand and Dai said to Maldwin, "'ave you seen my talking clock on the wall?" Maldwin said, "That's not a talking clock," and Dai said, "It is," and Maldwin said, "No it isn't." Anyway, our Dai started to thump the clock on the wall real hard like and then all of a sudden Elsie shouted through the wall from next door, "For God's sake Dai, it's five and twenty past two in the morning!"

Thursday

Our Philll must be ordering a Jeep on the 'phone. I heard him saying that he wanted a 10 by 8. He's doing so well with his surgery – there's always someone coming back and fore. He's definitely the ring leader in that business.

Mind you, Dai and me had a funny time in sin city today. We were in town doing a bit of shopping and Dai saw this traffic warden putting a ticket on the windscreen. So Dai says, "Come on buddy, what about giving a guy a break?" The traffic warden ignored him and carried on writing it out, so Dai called him a piece of horse manure. So the traffic warden wrote out another ticket and stuck it on the windscreen. Well, the more Dai abused him, the more tickets he put on the car. Mind you, Dai didn't mind, our car was parked around the corner.

The three Spanish boys, that's Rapheal, Rex and Paco, are going back to Spain to see their parents for Xmas. Shantelll, Elsie and Philll told them to all 'ave a bit of fun but 'ave warned them not to come back here without a cart load of fags.

Our Dai 'ave had a load of booze on the knock from a fella that delivers beer to the club. Mind you, he gave our Shantelll a big massive magnum of Champain and he didn't even charge her for it. She must 'ave done a bit of sewing for the boys.

Friday

Philll, Elsie and Shantelll are going up the club tonight because their partners 'ave all gone back to Spain and there's a strip show there tonight. Aw, it'll take our Philll's mind off work. I'm sure he's got a lot to put up with in that surgery and his hands are red raw. I told him straight, "Your hands 'ave got chaps on them. You should try and use a bit of cream on them." That'll make life a lot easier for him.

The steward of the club was in a tither. He had run out of whiskey and Bacardi, so our Dai nips home and lent him a couple of bottles. He's as good as gold. Mind you, I'm quite happy to sit here and sip my pint of Dark and 'ave a game of bingo.

Do you know? I can't wait for Xmas. It's going to be fantastic this year. We 'ave decided to go to the Halps for the Xmas 'olidays. Shantelll 'ave had a few presents already, but she seems a bit disappointed with them, so I told her, "Now Shantelll, be grateful, it's not the size that counts." But she wouldn't 'ave it.

I must tell you, our milk man, the one that 'ave just left his wife, 'ave given us free milk for six months. Aw love him and he's got such a bad back. Never mind, Philll will sort him out. He've had a few sessions already with him.

Christmas on the Piste

HELLO MY LOVELIES. It's Gladys here with the 'appenings from the Halps and we've been on the piste for nearly three weeks over the Xmas 'olidays. Marvellous.

The first day we got there we were met by a lovely young man called Fritz, he had a lovely figure and Philll chose him to be his instructor for the 'oliday. The three Spaniards were in Spain visiting their families, so Philll and Shantelll were on the loose and were going for it big time. Dai didn't leave the hotel, he was pouting because they couldn't find a ski suit big enough for him. Idwal went with us and had a ball and so did Philll!!!!

Vilhelm, the other ski instructor, asked Shantelll if she wanted to try a ski jump. Well she couldn't wait, she was off in a second. Mind you, goodness knows what she wanted an air bed for. Then they went up in a cable car to get to the top of the ski slope and it got stuck. There must 'ave been a terrible wind, the cable car was rocking back and fore like the clappers.

Anyway, on the second day Dai fancied some Swiss food and ordered a Swiss roll, damn he enjoyed it. Our Idwal met up with an old American dame, loaded she was and he told her that he was a count and showed her his Garden badge. She was well impressed and invited him to dinner the next day.

There was no sign of Shantelll. She was still stuck up in the cable car. I'm sure she found something to occupy her mind, she's such a good girl.

Philll had his first skyng lesson and he had a bit of trouble going in a straight line, he couldn't keep his legs together. He's doing so much exercise in the surgery, he's like a bendy toy. Philll and his instructor Fritz were about to go up the mountain to ski down and it was a long way up, so I told him in front of Fritz, "You'll never get up there love, you'll find it very hard my boy."

Later on that week Maxine Roxanne had a funny tummy and when we went into the buffet in the night she spewed up all over the table. Mind you, the waitresses were lovely and they moved us straight away and cleaned the table. I had some of the pineapple chunks I nicked from the club, so I left them on the table after she had cleaned it. A little while later our Idwal's lady friend, the old broad from America, came on to me and said, "Don't bother going into that restaurant, the fruit salad is as hard as nails. I'll take you all out for a meal somewhere else."

We had a 'phone call from our Gareth and he was saying that he wasn't getting on very well with his wife Cherylll. Mind you, she's an 'orrible cow and he was telling me that she used to be great in bed, but now she's starting to wake up at night. Poor boy!!!!!!

Well, I've got to tell you that our Dai had a lovely hair cut in the hotel. The barber's name was Herr Kuttt. Nice boy too!

There was no sign of Shantelll. She must have been exploring unseen parts or something.

Dai told his mate Maldwin to fetch him some fags back from his 'oliday as he went on 'oliday too and he don't smoke.

We tried desperately to find a penguin for Maxine Roxanne but couldn't find one anywhere.

Idwal really hit it off with this yankee millionaire piece and she threatened to come back with us. She thinks that he's a count. She'll 'ave a shock when she sees Ponty Pantin. If she likes it, her and Idwal can put in for a council house. There's two going up the road and they'll get it no problem. Shantelll will see to that, she's owed favours all over.

In the second week our Philll got a bit of the old hyper thermies while him and Fritz were stuck on a ski slope, so our Philll suggested that Fritz got into the sleeping bag with him so that he could keep warm. Duw, I'm glad that I sent him to Saint Jims Ambulance when he was a kid. You never know when unforeseen things could pop up. I made him take an air bed with him as well. Well, you never know when you might want to 'ave a kip in it. But I warned him, "Take some patches with you, it might get punchered." I told him straight, "If that thing goes down on you, you'll be blowing for ever."

Anyway, the Swiss authorities sent an helicopter up to see if Shantelll and Vilhelm were OK in the cable car, but the windows were all misted up. It's the temperature you see.

Dai found a telly lounge in the hotel and retuned the moving satellite dish so all the residents could watch *Wales Today* and SC4 the Welsh. They all felt at home then.

I bought some lovely presents for the family, especially Elsie. I bought her some magnifying goggles from the ski shop, so she can see to her gas meter instead of having to Sellotape her glasses on. Very handy I thought.

I warned Philll about going out with not enough clothes on. I told him straight, "Carry on like that my boy and you'll be covered in chaps."

They eventually got Shantelll out of the cable car, mind you, not without a struggle and the poor instructor looked knackerated. I think he was glad to get down, after all, he'd been up quite a while and with it being so cold it must 'ave been very hard for Shantelll.

Anyway, the old dame from America is coming over to join our Idwal. She's got to go back to America first to dump her husband. Well, I thought, fair enough. I'll 'ave to 'ave a word with our Shantelll to get the ball rolling for a council house. She's made that much contact with people from working in the surgery. She can 'ave just about anything.

So here I am packing away to go home and I can't find Philll and Shantelll anywhere to help me. If they've gone out on the piste again there'll be uproar. But oh that Dai's a mucky pup. He keeps shoving packages in our Maxine Roxanne's suitcase. I'm sure he's bought me some surprises.

Maldwin 'ave texted me on the mobile, he 'ave had fags

from his 'oliday. I texted him back and asked, "Where did you go Maldwin?" He texted back, "Blackpool."

Anyway, we landed back in sin city tidy, but the trouble was with the suitcases. No sign of them. Our Maxine Roxanne went around the conveyor belt twice to look for them. They did come at last and then there it was, Her Majesties Customs!!!!!!!!!!

We goes through and sure as eggs, they stopped our Dai. "Anything to declare sir?" the blokie asked. "No," says our Dai. He opened the suitcase and counted 18,000 fags. The man said, "Are these yours?" and our Dai said, "They are all for my personal contradiction." It was just as well that our Idwal had a bad turn and the customs let us through.

Dai

On the Gower
* WEEK 1 *

HIYA LOVES, IT'S GLADYS here with the 'appenings that 'ave 'appened here in wonderful Ponty Pantin and what a time we had in the Halps. Dai 'ave brought a lot of Swiss rolls back to give as presents. He's such a darling. Here goes...

Saturday

The dog Christopher/Christine hasn't been well, so I am taking him to the vets today to 'ave him checked out. He's such a worry to us as we all love him/her dearly.

Dai 'ave had the runs since he 'ave come back from the Halps. Mind you, it's good exercise for him, otherwise he'd never shift.

Shantelll is planning on going out tonight with Philll because the Spaniards are still away, so look out tonight in the club.

Philll 'ave double booked a few clients in his surgery, but he reckons he'll fit them all in. He's done in, love him. Boy has he got his hands full. I've never seen so many bad backs in my life. Oh I'm so proud of our Philll being a qualified massewer.

We all goes up the club in the night and Shantelll has put on her new pelmet. That's what Dai calls her mini skirts anyway, and Philll has got his new rubber outfit on. Damn they look smart. I went as well, well you've got to try your luck at the bingo 'aven't you? So I've had six books and I mark them upside down not to be bored.

A fella turned up in the lounge bar with some car batteries for sale, a tenner each. So we had six of them just in case there was a power cut. We get them a lot in Ponty Pantin mind. And I had some lovely fish from behind the bar. Beautiful it was. The only thing, Philll isn't fussed on fish. He's more of a meat eater, love him.

Philll got plastered and so did Shantelll and they decided to go to a club in town, so off they scoots, leaving me with Dai in the club. I called the snowball – £150. Oh I was landed and off we went home happy as Larry.

The dog's in the vets and he's staying in over night, God love him!!!

Sunday

Well it must 'ave been about twenty past six in the morning when Philll and Shantelll came home and they had two fellas with them. Well, I mean to say, what does Shantelll want with two men? Fair play, our Philll didn't 'ave a girl with him. She should take·a leaf out of his book: pure in mind and in body. Mind you they seemed nice boys. They weren't related, you could tell. One was quite hunky, looked like a builder and the other one was quite slight with pink trousers and a frilly top on. They asked if they could stay for a while as they had been up all night and they wanted a rest before they went home. So the builder chap slept in our Shantelll's room and the other little lad went into our Philll's room. Our Philll is so good letting that boy kip in his room. I mean to say, Shantelll's room is so small, she wouldn't know which way to turn with both of them in there.

Around about dinner time the boys came out of the bedrooms and they looked worse for wear. They were sweating pints and looked like they'd been on a ten-mile hike. I've told our Idwal about leaving the central heating on overnight.

Anyway, off they went and we all sat down to Sunday dinner. Shantelll fancied fish fingers and Philll wanted a jumbo sausage. Well, I mean to say on a Sunday as well. Idwal 'ave recorded Dewi Griffiths, we never miss that and Shantelll loves that *String of Pearls*. She often talks about it to Philll.

We've got to go and get the dog tomorrow. I hope he'll be alright.

Monday

'Phoned the vet first thing and had some terrible news. The dog has died. Well I didn't know what to do. I was grief stricked. How was I going to tell the family? Idwal, well you'd expect, but the dog, never!

Anyway, I sat them down and told them the dog has gone to a better place. Dai thought I'd farmed him out to some other family, but when they all realised, they were all so very upset.

Philll and Shantelll started the arrangements straight away and we wanted him buried in the garden next to the surgery. Mind you, the vet delivered our Christopher in a lovely box all proper like. So fair play, Philll and Shantelll worked wonders. They had flowers done and hymn sheets as well and as we buried our lovely dog in the garden, we all sung 'A four-legged friend' with our karaoke machine. Duw, it was so moving!

Then we had a little buffet and all our friends that had animals came and gave Christopher a good send off. Duw it's going to be hard now bringing up those three puppies on our own. Well, I mean to say, we're all God's children ain't we?

That night we felt terrible and we couldn't even put the telly on just in case that Rolf Harris was on with the animal programme. But they say every cloud has a silver lining. Dai found a chap up the club to buy the dog basket. Fair play, he had twenty quid for it.

Tuesday

Things will never be the same again without our Christopher. Dai's brother Willy said he could get a lovely little dog and he'd bring it around to show us. So Willy turns up with a dog, or should I say a monster, a Great Dane. As if we 'aven't got enough to cope with, what with the three puppies. But we fell in love with him straight away. We were all trying like mad to come up with a name for him. Philll wanted Cledwyn, Shantelll wanted Keannu, so I comprimises and the dog is called Cledwyn Keannu – that'll stop the arguments.

Meanwhile Idwal 'ave had a letter from this American piece he met while out in the Halps to say that she's coming over to stay for a couple of weeks.

Thinking about it, I'm sure the shock of Christopher finding out that he was a female killed him. Anyway, life goes on.

Wednesday

The Spaniards are back today, Rapheal, Rex and Paco and I've got to admit I'm so glad that Rex is back 'cause our Elsie next door 'ave been keeping on how empty she feels without him there. Wait until they see the new dog Cledwyn Keannu.

I must admit that Cledwyn Keannu has settled in tidy, but he takes up a lot of room. I wonder if the council will give us a bigger house? Shantelll seems to think they might, they owe her a couple of favours, probably a bit more sewing she's done I should imagine.

Anyway, the Spanish boys trundled in with loads of suitcases and I'm glad to say they were full of fags. Philll and Shantelll were landed. Shantelll said to her beloved husband, "Oh I'm glad you're back. I'm fed up of sitting in the house all the time. I'll be glad to go out somewhere with you." She then disappeared upstairs with 40 cartons. Paco then scoots upstairs straight after her, aw there's love for you. Then Shantelll said to him, "There you are love. I've changed the bed clothes especially for you." Aw she's a good girl mind.

Idwal has started to take vitamins ready for his new American lady friend. He reckons he'll need all the strength he can muster. His motto is 'Keep them happy, and they'll leave you everything'!!!!!!

Anyway the 'phone goes and it's the vet, but I couldn't talk to him. I was too upset. It's too early yet, I'm still in shock to be honest. So I puts the 'phone down on him and later on the in the day Shantelll said to me, "There's a message on the answerphone from the vet to ring him straight away." But I left it, I couldn't face it.

Thursday

There's a bang on the door, but now we've got it sussed, we don't hide things anymore in case it's the Social. We've got a camera outside so we can see who is outside the door and it was the vet. I opens the door and there stands the vet with Christopher. He'd messed up the files. What he'd sent us was a box of animal hair after clipping him. Well I was dumb struck, mind you, we were so glad to see our Christopher back with us. Dai had a go at the vet and wanted compo for the pain and suffering and the sandwiches, and fair play he paid up straight away – enough for another 'oliday.

I said to our Christopher, "Don't you go and die on Mammy again." God I hope that Christopher and Cledwyn Keannu get on with each other. This house is getting too small for us: Philll, Shantelll, Rapheal, Paco, Idwal, me, Dai, two dogs, three puppies and Willy on the weekend.

I've just thought, if Cledwyn Keannu, the Great Dane and Christopher, the female half-Jack Russell get together, we could call the puppies Jane Russells.

Friday

Well I don't know where to turn. We are buying a marquay for out the back for extra space. Cadwalider is back today with Shantelll, he's been staying down with Cherylll, my daughter-in-law, for a while, while Shantelll was out sewing her oats. I didn't know that she liked porridge so much.

Idwal is like a dog on heat, waiting for this American piece to arrive. She's a millionairess and I'm sure they'll hit it off. He's going out today with our Shantelll to see if he can 'ave a flat off the council.

Shantelll really enjoyed that trip to the Halps, she said the best thing was the ski jump, and boy does she know how to make a Swiss roll.

Anyway darlings 'ave a fab weekend. I'll catch you next week, and as they say in Ponty Pantin, if I don't see you again it'll be too soon and if you're ever passing this way, keep passing. Tara loves…

On the Gower
* WEEK 2 *

WELL HELLO MY LOVELIES, how are you?

I hopes you are keeping half-tidy and you are keeping warm. Oh Idwal is so handy to keep around the house. We gets loads of 'lectric because of his age, and we finally got the free telly license in his name 'cause he told the post office he's over 75. Elsie's going spare 'cause she's going 'ave to get her own. Oh it's good to 'ave an old gripper about the place innit? Anyway, what a week this week. The key word this week is Mumbles! Look out...

Saturday

The old dame, the millionairess from America that's knocking around with our Idwal, has gone and bought a mansion down the Mumbles, and to be honest she's loosing it a bit. I means she can't remember nothing. Shantelll has been working on her to let us all stay with her in Swansea, mind you if Shantelll gets her own way she'll 'ave the mansion signed over to us in a jiffy. She's a marvellous girl mind.

Philll has been away over the weekend, I think it's something to do with a fishing trip. He's back later on. I hope he's enjoyed himself.

Anyway, we're all down the mansion at the moment and we're trying to decide which rooms to 'ave for ourselves. I decided to 'ave a front room bedroom, overlooking the works in Port Talbot. Our Dai used to get lovely soap from there, carbolic, you could wash the step with it lovely and wash yourself tidy with it. Aw those were the days. I been busy putting pineapple chunks into the new mansion, it smells lush now. Home from home. To be honest, I hope Idwal marries this American piece, I fancy this house rotten.

Next thing, Philll enters the room, back from his fishing trip and boy, did he 'ave his hands full of goodies. He had trout for Dai and bass for me, so I says to him, "What did you get for yourself love?" "Crabs Mam, just crabs," he said. I warned him, "Make sure they are fresh, otherwise you'll be up all night."

Sunday

Our Philll has had an early start today. He has got a load of clients this morning, the poor dabs. Must 'ave terrible bad backs, to come on a Sunday.

Anyway, he was hard at it down the surgery, so I thought I'd cut him a plate of sandwiches. He 'aven't had so much as a nibble yet today. So I leaves the sandwiches outside the surgery with a bit of cling film over the top, just in case the ferret pees on them. About ten minutes later the sarnies were gone. Aw, I thought to myself, he must 'ave devoured them. So I knocks on the door and says, "Philll? Do you want anything else to eat?" Philll mumbled, "No, it's OK Mam." I told him straight not to speak with his mouth full. Naughty boy!

Idwal 'ave just come into the house with some shocking news. Him and the American dame are getting married. I thinks to myself, yes, Gladys, that mansion is getting closer.

Monday

The old American dame is coming up to see us today in Ponty Pantin, so I'd better treat her right. Anyway, in she comes, mutton dressed as lamb. So I says to her, "Do you want a cup of tea love?" and she says back to me, "Oh yes please. I love the tea in England." I thought to myself, say nothing about England, keep her sweet. So I says, "This is a lovely part of England isn't it? You've got the windy city, well we've got Wales, the wet county of England." Keep her sweet, keep her sweet.

Then she says to me that she only wants a small wedding: just a few horse-drawn carriages and a few grenadier guards and about 400 guests. Well, I thought to myself, this will be interesting.

Shantelll enters the room and calls me to one side. She said to me, "Look Mam, the old dame has given me £1,000 for me to 'ave a life saving operation and Mam, I'm not preggers. The doctor had the wrong notes." Do you know I can't keep up with this family.

The next thing Maxine Roxanne comes in with her homework. They were doing poetry in school so I says to her to tell Gramma what poems she had written. So Maxine Roxanne reads it out: "Mary had a little lamb/she tied it to a pylon/a massive volt went up its butt/and turned it into nylon."

Aw, I can see it all now. She'll be in the Eisteddfod before long.

Tuesday

Idwal and the old dame are busy making plans for their wedding. Our Idwal says, "At our ages you've got to move pretty sharpish like." Anyway, I'm leaving them to get on with it, mind you she 'ave given our Dai's Willy three grand to get a few things for the wedding. I can see disaster striking here before long.

Shantelll 'ave just written a lovely letter to her ex boyfriend. She wrote:

Dear Jim,

I cannot sleep at night thinking about you. I miss you so much I can't eat either.

Nobody is as good as you and I really do believe that I 'ave married the wrong man.

Can you find it in your heart to forgive me and maybe we can try again?

You are a fantastic man in and out of bed. I love you with all of my heart. Oh and by the way, congratulations on winning the lottery last week.

Anyway, I goes to visit my old friend out in the sticks in

Gwent and I gets off the bus and walks past this lovely old cottage with a front porch on it. There was an old gent sitting in a rocking chair happy as the day, smiling like the clappers. So as I walks past I says to him, "Why are you so happy?" He says, "My secret is not working, drinking three cases of cider a night, smoking 100 fags a day and doing no exercise at all." "Well," I said, "that's fantastic. How old are you?" He said, "26."

Wednesday

We had a lovely dinner today, pork, and I told our Maxine Roxanne to eat all her pork. "Go on," I says to her, "it's cured." She said back to me, "It looks dead to me, Gran."

The dogs, I'm glad to say, are down the mansion with their own butler. Life seems to be getting better.

Philll is going in for a little operation today. Men's trouble down below. He said to me, "Mam, I might not be back until tomorrow." I told him straight, "There's no skin off my nose love."

The old dame, who is called Netty by her friends in America, is settling in nicely. Dai 'ave told Netty about a dead cert on the gee gees and she's putting £500 each way on a horse. I've never seen Dai so happy.

Thursday

Cadwalider 'ave spewed up all over the parlour floor and Shantelll's not here to clean it up so muggings will do it, I suppose. I told her not to give him four breasts of lamb for dinner, even if she did liquidise 'em.

Idwal is taking Netty up to the club tonight for a game of bingo. She's never played it before. Dai told her, "It's customary in Wales for the guest to buy the bingo books." He's not daft.

Do you know it's always the same: money goes to money. She called two full houses, four lines and she won the raffle, a big box of chocolates.

She went to the toilet and she went into the gents by

mistake and when she came out she said, "Those toilets are very awkward to sit on here and everybody can see you, and they smell just like your house Gladys – like pineapples."

I thinks to myself, let's get her out of here before she drops me right in it. So we takes her for a Chinese up the road. Aw they're lovely boys and they made a fabluss fuss over Netty and do you know what? She gave them a £100 tip.

I hope to God that Idwal marries her before she kicks the bucket.

Friday

Philll is home from the hospital and he seems OK, but very sore. The doctor 'ave told him not to get excited otherwise he could bust his stitches. So anyway, he's settling down for the night to watch telly and he said to me, "Don't worry Mam. I'll be OK. I'm watching Miss World."

Elsie and Rex 'ave been out in the car for a run and when they got back they noticed they had a punchure. So there was Rex mending the wheel and in comes Elsie for a cuppa. I asks her, "How are things with you and Rex?" "Oh," she said, "things couldn't be better, but he's wearing me out. He don't stop. So I said to him, 'Get outside and blow that tyre up – that'll be a change for you.' He's around me all day. He won't leave me alone. He started getting frisky with me down the Co-op by the frozen veg, well I mean to say…"

Anyway, time to get up the wooden hill and get some shut eye. The only thing is, there's a terrible racket coming from Elsie's next door. They must be moving furniture, or he's building shelves. I don't know, but there's definitely something up there.

On the Gower
* WEEK 3 *

WELL HELLO MY LOVELIES. How are you this week? Well it's all go here. Idwal has decided to marry Netty the old American dame and they are getting married on weds this week. Look out, Elsie's brawn will be flying. Here goes...

Saturday

Idwal came down the stairs and announced that he was getting married. He said, "I can't leave it much longer, she might kick the bucket and where would that leave me?" So I tells him not to worry, we will sort it all out and it'll be fabs.

I gets hold of our Dai's brother Willy and he said that he would get a cake sorted, mind you, the old dame told us not to spare the expense. Go for gold and she would pay for everything.

She wants the reception here in the village, so guess where we are having it? Yes, up the club and the wedding itself will take place in the regie office down in sin city. Her brother is coming over as well to be at the wedding, he's 98 years old and he's got a wife of 24. Can you believe it??

Anyway, I nips up the doctors and sits in the waiting room, waiting for my turn to come and there was quite a few waiting I must admit. So next thing, in comes this fella with a suit on and a brief case, looks around the room and barges in towards the doctor's room. So I says to him, "Oi love, why don't you wait your turn? I'm before you." And he says back to me, "No lady, I'm before you, I'm the doctor."

Sunday

Netty is out today with Idwal looking for a new dress to wear for the wedding. She wants something in beige so it will match her brown teeth through smoking. She wants Shantelll as matron of honour and Philll is pouting because he wanted that role. He's always been sensitive mind.

Cadwalider is wearing his leather biker's jacket. He's six months now and damn he looks a right bobby dazzler with his pierced ears and all. Dai will wear his usual old faithful suit he had from the charity shop. It does for funerals, court cases, everything.

Anyway, Shantelll was out shopping with her gorgeous Spanish husband and the car broke down in the car park outside the supermarket. So he said, "Go on in Shantelll and do the shopping and I'll get under the car and mend it in time for you to go home." Anyway, there was a hell of a stir outside the supermarket. There was a crowd of people all staring at two legs sticking out from under the car and the trousers had split and everyone could see this man's privates. So Shantelll rushed up to the car and covered the exposed parts and put them out of sight. Well the next thing, Paco taps her on the shoulder and said, "I called the breakdown service, he's under there now." Boy, did he 'ave a lump on his head.

Monday

The wedding is on Wednesday and to be fair the old dame 'ave seen to it all, but we've got to pick up the brother from the airport in London of all places. Anyway, down goes Malcolm the taxis to pick him up and he was holding a card saying 'By here Yank'.

Anyway, this big Texan walks through the arrivals with a cowboy hat on like JR and cowboy boots, the whole works. So they sits in the taxi and the American started bragging, so Malcolm starts retaliating. They went past the Tower of London and Mal says, "They started construction of this in 1346 and completed it in 1412." The Texan said, "Blow that, we built a skyscraper in the States in two weeks." So Malcolm says back to him, "There's the Houses of Parliament, construction started in 1544 and completed in 1618." The Texan said, "We put a bigger one up in Dallas and it only took us a year." Then they passed Westminster Abbey and the

Texan said, "What's that over there?" Our Malcolm said, "I don't know, it wasn't there yesterday."

Tuesday

The Texan, Waylon is his name, is staying in the Inn and Out up in Ponty Pantin and he's done nothing but complain: "Everything is so small here."

Mind you, our Shantelll is as cool as a cucumber and she's going to do a jigsaw. So I left her to it in the front room. Next thing I could hear a load of bad language and there was our Shantelll ranting and raving. I said, "What is it supposed to be?" She said, "It's got a picture of a cockerel on the box and I can't do it." I said to her, "Put those corn flakes away before our Christopher gets hold of them."

Philll 'ave had to cancel a few of his clients this week. I hope he can make ends meet. But I'm so proud of that boy, never mind if he finds himself in a hole, he'll always get out of it.

The wedding is tomorrow, I can't wait, any excuse to 'ave a flagon of cider and I love them volovonts with paste in. Our Elsie does lovely ones from up the Co-op.

Wednesday

The big day has arrived and the American bloke, Waylon, has hired a big convertible car, so we all piles in and sits tidy in the back with our sandwiches and off we goes to the regie office. Well, if you saw the state of the old dame, she had a leopard skin tight skirt on with a see through top. Dai said the last time he saw a botty like that it had a saddle on it and that her top half looked like a map of the Brecon Beacons.

Anyway, the minister chappy said, "Do you Idwal Maldwin Al Jolson Jenkins take this woman to be your lawful wedded wife?" Our Id said, "Aye." Then the minister said to Netty, "Do you Nesta Dolores Ewing take this man to be your lawful wedded husband?" She says, "Sure honey."

Well I couldn't help myself from crying tears of joy. At last I've got that mansion and my future is secure.

We all went back to the club and it looked a picture. Idwal put a picture of the queen over the bar and Elsie had made lovely paste sandwiches for us all. Waylon said he likes it here and might stay for a while. He said, "This is a lovely part of England." I said nothing, but I could see that a few of the locals didn't like it. I told them to shut their traps: "There's money on the way, they are both multi-millionaires." So old Joe from Ponty Pantin said to the Texan, "If you want I'll take you out and show you the sights of this lovely county of England. I only charge £250." Waylon jumped at the idea and booked the trip straight away.

Thursday

Idwal and Netty 'ave gone on honeymoon. They've gone to Anglesey, the Majorca of Wales – in England of course! Well you've got to pacify them 'aven't you?

Waylon said to Dai, "Do you know Dai, you can get on a train in Texas in the morning, ride all day and still be in Texas in the night!" Dai said back to him, "I knows what you means, we've got slow trains here as well."

Cadwalider looked lush yesterday in his biker's jacket. I can't wait to see the photos, mind you, most of the photos were done when we were playing bingo, that's the only time the photographer could get us all together and quiet.

Friday

Philll's stitches are coming out today, you know the other week he had a little op down below. So off he goes to the doctor for a check up and as the doctor was examining him, Philll sang, "You've got the whole world in your hands," and the doctor sang back, "There goes your only possession, there goes your everything."

Philll is having a new number plate on his car today. It's BENT 1. I think it stands for 'best-ever natural treatment'.

On the Gower
* WEEK 4 *

WELL HELLO MY LOVELIES, it's Gladys here with the 'appenings that 'ave 'appened here in Ponty Pantin. The weather has been awful, especially when them Yanks are here looking around at everything. Anyway, I must tell you about the driving lessons, just you wait. Anyway here goes...

Saturday

The Americans are still here, well Waylon anyway. Netty and Idwal 'ave gone to Anglesey for their honeymoon, the Costa del Gog, and Waylon 'ave been paying a fortune to the locals to show him around this lovely part of England. He thinks Wales is a county of England, but at £250 a trip, he can call it Poland if he wants.

Dai 'ave had a letter to go and see the Social on Monday, they're giving him an increase because of his incurable bad back. I wanted him to go to our Philll's surgery, but Philll said he doesn't do family members.

Me and Dai are having a night in tonight and the rest of them are out on the town, so Dai is watching the snooker in the living room and I'm watching a weepy video in the front room. We've always been a couple that does things together.

Sunday

I was up first thing and made my way down to the mansion in Swansea and who did I bump into? That lovely Bonnie Tyler and she says to me, "Moved in recent 'ave you love?" So I says, "Yes Bonnie, my son is a famous and wealthy doctor. He would 'ave loved to 'ave met you, but he's busy this morning seeing to someone's back side." So then I told her if she wants to pop in for a brawn sandwich she's always welcome.

I've just noticed the lovely out houses in the grounds of the mansion, they must be the places where Philll wants to start another surgery. He 'ave always said he'd be quite willing to open up in Swansea.

Anyway off I scoots home to get a bit of dinner ready and when I gets home Shantelll is hard at it with the Highway Code. She 'ave passed her written exam, but tomorrow is going to be the one, the driving test itself. She's all prepared: low top, tiny mini skirt and her uplift bra. She reckons that's all she'll needs. She's so confident.

Monday

Shantelll has gone down the surgery with our Philll and Simon. She's got a few clients to see to before she goes on her driving test. Damn she looks smart in her nurses uniform. She do turn some heads believe you me. Dear me, there must be some with a terrible bad back, the moans and groans from down there is unbelievable.

Anyway our Shantelll sets off. Malcolm took her to the test centre and she looked a picture in her tight little outfit, all legs and teeth. Anyway, in she goes to the waiting room and out comes this young blokie and says, "Miss Shantelll Toyah Angharad Jenkins." She says, "Wow, hello," and in the car they went and off they drove about 11 o'clock. Malcolm sat in the waiting room. Anyway, other people were pulling back in and there was no sign of our Shantelll. They gets back in about 20 past one and she's passed. They'd been down some country lanes in the Vale apparently and I warned her not to leave the top of the car down. You should 'ave seen the mess on the blokie's hair. You could swear he'd been 20 rounds with Tyson. I says to her, "How do you feel Shantelll?" And she said to me, "Knackered Mam, knackered." I've always known she's had some hidden talents. Ooh, I'm chuffed for her. The examiner blokie says it was the best ride he's had in years.

Tuesday

Idwal and Netty are coming back today from the Costa del

Gog and they look great. So I says to her, "How did you enjoy it love?" and she says to me, "How did you know?"

This has got to be the best story yet: Netty is 76 and thinks she's preggers. You know she's not quite all there, so we are all pacifying her and sending her congratulation cards, just to keep the piece. I can't cope with all of this.

Anyway, Dai goes up the club and he was having a drink by the bar and this mobile 'phone starts ringing. So this blokie picks it up and puts it on loudspeaker so that everyone could hear. This woman said on the 'phone, "Can I 'ave that dress I saw last week, the one that cost £400?" The blokie said, "Yes love, 'ave two." Then the woman asks, "Can I 'ave that new Mercy that I saw last week?" The blokie said, "Yes love, make it a convertible." Then the woman said, "Can I book a world cruise?" "Yes go ahead," he told her. Then he switched off the 'phone and said, "Does anyone know whose 'phone this is?" Well I mean to say, the cheek of some people.

Wednesday

Shantelll has gone out and bought herself a new car, one with a lid on it that opens up like, and she 'ave got her own private number plate on it. Well she's always got to keep up with Philll 'asn't she? What was the number now? Oh yes, SLA G1, damn it looks fab and it suits her I must admit.

Anyway, she's now doing a mobile service for people with bad backs and she's already made a start. She's off down sin city, to someone on the bay. Well they can afford private treatment down there can't they? They're always going on 'olidays and having new cars, not like us poor people here in Ponty Pantin. She got an appointment with a doctor, mind you, goodness knows what treatment he wants. He must 'ave a bad back and he can't get round to it.

I'm so glad that my children are doing so well. They are so polite, they always rise to the occasion.

Thursday

That Netty has really lost it. She's now asking us if she can stay in Ponty Pantin and says we can go down the mansion

Gladys

Idwal

Dai

Philll

Shantelll

Jason

Chris Needs 'The Jenkins's's's's's'

I'm afraid we do not think you are educationally equipped to fill the position of this job.

Fantastic news, Dai! Mrs Daviesss has just been blessed with a newborn grandson!

First of all, where it says 'sign' on the application form, you wrote 'Aquarius'.

I wonder when our Philll will give us a grandchild of our own?

However we were more concerned about you sending your application by fax

Erm... well this is only a guess....

Sending a fax? modern technology? What's the problem?

...but I don't think it will be any time soon!

You put a stamp on it!

Yoo-hoo! See you tomorrow, Mam, Gonna go down to the Blue Oyster Bar with the boys for a gay old time!

Your mother has been complaining that we don't spend enough time togther...

...and there's nothing like good old-fashioned sports to bond a father and son together...

So what do you want to do? Football? Rugby? Wrestling?

Once this is over, me and you need to have a **serious** chat!

People think that ferrets ar dirty, disgusting, evil and nasty animals!

But in actual fact, they can be lovable, friendly, loyal and caring pets!

Isn't that right Jason, my beautiful little baby?

I swear to GOD!! Tonight I'm gonna kill you in your sleep!

and live there. Well, about 5 minutes later when I was nearly packed, the doorbell rang, so I checks the outside with the camera and lo and behold it's the Social. So I opens the door and they had a letter. Dai had forgotten to go down there for his visit. Anyway, to cut a long story short, they gave me a new book with an increase on it. Good old Shantelll had 'phoned them and said that her dad was in too much pain to go himself. Wow I thought, that was a lucky one!

I gave our Shantelll the pick of the rooms in the mansion for being so good and sorting us out. She is going to convert the cellar and turn it into another surgery. She 'ave had some lovely mirrors put in all around and on the ceiling. Well, when you're painting nails you need to see what you are doing I suppose. I know that the dogs misbehave, but I think she's gone too far with those whips.

Friday

Well, we are all settled in the new mansion and Netty and Idwal are happy living up in Ponty Pantin. It's the bright lights for us now you know, and talking of which there's a few nice red ones hanging outside. Damn they look nice in the night. You can stand outside the mansion and the view of the works in Port Talbot is wonderful.

We're having a house warming party tonight but we're not inviting Netty, just in case she remembers how nice her house is. Philll 'ave invited a load of his clients and Shantelll 'ave invited quite a few as well, including the blokie she went on her driving test with. I'm glad to see that he 'ave combed his hair this time.

Elsie and Rex 'ave come down here to stay, well the house is so big and she's renting out her council house and she makes about £25 a week above the rent of it. Now that's what I call enterprising. I can't believe the amount of weight she's put on since she's been with Rex. I can't understand it. He must be filling her with that Spanish sausage.

On the Gower
* WEEK 5 *

WELL HELLO MY LOVELIES. Here we are again: the Jenkins's's's's's from Ponty Pantin, now living in the Mumbles. Good old Netty. Well I hope you're sitting comfortably, if so, I'll begin.

Saturday

What a day, bookies slips all over the place. Dai reckons he's got a dead cert on the go. The only thing certain for him is about 12 pints of Dark tonight. Mind you, he misses the club so we're all off to a posh nightclub in Swansea tonight. I hope they've got bingo on there. Elsie, who's now living with us in the mansion in the Mumbles wants to go to the Dockers Club. She said they do tidy bingo there, so you never know.

Do you know I'm sat here looking at our Dai and he 'aven't changed much. In fact, he's still wearing the same vest he had on for our wedding. It's gone a bit grey now, I'll 'ave to try and get a clothes grant off the Social for him. Well you 'ave to look your best when you live in a mansion down the Mumbles don't you? I never forget the time he proposed to me all them years ago. He went down on one knee and said, "Gladys, will you marry me?" But the trouble is they 'ave a skin full and forget by the morning don't they? He drinks so much he can pee in the tank of the car and still get back from work to 'ave his dinner.

Philll has moved his surgery down here to Swansea and he's booked up solid. I told him, "You'll be wearing yourself out my boy." He never listens to me. I told his friend Rapheal to take him in hand.

Anyway, we've decided to give the nightclub a miss tonight. Shantelll is getting a take away instead for us. She nipped down to the local Chinese and brought us back a lovely selection of grub and some knitting needles to eat it with.

Sunday

Rapheal is cooking paella for us today. I don't know what Dai will say about that. Shantelll said she'd prefer meat and two veg. She's landed mind, now that she's passed her test. New car, private number plate and all posh mind. I've just pressed her nurses uniform because she's got to assist Philll in the surgery later on this evening. Anyway, the paella was lush and Shantelll made us some cocktails. She made us a David and Goliath – one drink and you're stoned. Marvellous.

Mind you, the doctor told our Dai, "The best thing for you Mr Jenkins is to give up drinking." Our Dai asked, "What's the second best?"

The ferret has been playing up a bit. He's not settling in to living in Swansea at all, so Shantelll has pasted some photos of Ponty Pantin in his cage. Aw, it's doing him good. Good old Shantelll.

Monday

Our Shantelll was very clever to pass her driving test the first time. Apparently, the examiner asked her all the right questions. He said, "Where can't you park?" She said in an erogenous zone, damn she's clever. She 'ave had a new mobile 'phone. Apparently she took some photos of the examiner during her test but she promised not to send them to his wife. Well he doesn't want to be seen with his hair in a mess does he now? She says it's the most handiest thing she 'ave had in years, next to uplift bras.

Anyway, we had a lovely tea today: plastic ham and chips, we've found a good chippy here no problem.

Rapheal is teaching us how to dance flamingo style, good job there's a wooden floor here, he would 'ave ruined the oil cloth in my other house.

Tuesday

Elsie 'ave had a letter from the council. As you know she's

renting out her council house and making about £25 a week profit. Well good luck to her, that's what I say and she's really happy with her new Spaniard Rex. He's up to all sorts and she's totally worn out. Anyway, the council want to know who the new people are in her house. So she's 'phoned them to tell them that they are relatives from away and she's letting them stay for a while. Mind you, Philll told her he's had words with someone in the housing department in the surgery and he said not to worry, things would be fine. Perhaps he doesn't want Philll to tell his employers that he's got a bad back. Love him.

Tuesday night Elsie's false teeth fell down the toilet. Rex didn't seem to mind that she'd lost her teeth, but she managed to get them out in the end. I asked her if they were alright. "Yes," she said, "I've given them a good clean."

Wednesday

Shantelll and Paco are taking salsa dancing lessons. Dai reckons there's more movement in our front room carpet. He said, "She looks like she's pushing a Hoover across the floor."

I've just had the council tax bill for the mansion, thank God that Netty is paying for it all. It's a lot of money for just six black bags and the water is on a meter here as well, so we all nips home to Ponty Pantin to 'ave a bath.

Tomorrow Dai and Shantelll are going to France for the day to get some fags.

Thursday

Dai and Shantelll 'ave gone for the day to foreign parts. I'll never understand why British fags are cheaper abroad. Roll on tonight. We'll 'ave a couple of cartons, lush. Mind you, I do miss the club. You can get anything you want there under the counter. They'll even change a cheque for you!

There's a massive conservatory here in the mansion, with a stone floor. You think the cheapskate would 'ave put a bit of carpet down. The dogs' paws get awful cold on the stone tiles. I'll 'ave to 'ave a word with Netty.

A lovely boy has just arrived to see our Philll, he looks quite fit mind, he doesn't seem to 'ave a bad back at all. Philll scuttled him in to the surgery, a lovely pink shirt he had on mind, looked lovely. He came out a bit later all smiling. I said to him, "Is everything all right love?" He said, "Yes thank you, I feel much better now. Can I pay with American Express?" I said to him, "Go as fast as you like love."

Friday

Dai's back with a cart load of fags and 'bacco and Shantelll has brought a load of Champain back with her. Well we need to entertain a bit now in this big posh house. Champain and brawn sandwiches. Lush!

Idwal is coming down tonight with Netty his new wife. When she smiles she reminds me of our Shantelll's horse, she's got the same teeth but stained with nicotine. She ought to soak her teeth in a drop of bleach, but the only trouble then is that beer goes flat in your mouth afterwards.

There's cartons of fags everywhere here and I'll 'ave to put them away so our Philll don't see them. He smokes too much for my liking. I said to him just the other day, "If you smoke much more, you'll turn in to a fag."

On the Gower
* WEEK 6 *

HIYA LOVES, IT'S GLADYS here with the 'appenings that 'ave 'appened this week. I hope you are all feeling well. Philll has got a cold and he's also got a bad elbow. I can't imagine where he's picked this lot up from. Anyway, here goes…

Saturday

Woke up bright and breezie. Dai had left the window open here in the mansion down in the Mumbles. It's strange you know, us living here in a posh big house and that Idwal and Netty living in our old house in Ponty Pantin. Mind you, I do miss the village terrible. I'd love to go back but this is the only chance I've got to keep up with the crachach.

Philll wants to buy a new flat down the bay in Cardiff, like that Charlotte Church and that Chris Needs 'ave. He reckons there's a lot of custom down the bay in sin city. He said there's a lot there waiting to be filled. Mind you, he's very good with his hands: all his patients leave with a smiling face, all the bad backs cured tidy.

Well 'aven't we done well? Philll looking for an apartment down in sin city bay, us in a mansion and Shantelll happily married and working hard as a nurse. I said to our Dai in bed this morning, "Give us a kiss love," and he said that by the time I find my teeth it'll be time to 'ave dinner.

Sunday

Philll is very exited – he's taking us down to see the new apartment in sin city bay. So we packs the usual, stacks of sandwiches and a couple of bottles of larger and off we sets, down the M4 heading for sin city.

I asks him when we got there, "Why do you want so many

bedrooms for?" There were four bedrooms. With that, this flussy of a fella the estate agent popped out of the kitchen with all the details of the apartment. Lovely plucked eyebrows he had. I think he must 'ave a few things in common with our Philll. They seemed to know each other well. Anyway, we all had a look around the place and Philll decided to buy it.

We left the two of them to it. They were gabbering like hell when we left, about a club in Cardiff. Our Philll do get himself into some tight spots you know. Anyway good luck to him.

Monday

The ferret is not settling in to the new mansion at all and we don't know what to do. I think that Idwal and Netty are going to 'ave to 'ave him back up there in Ponty Pantin.

Shantelll 'ave been out shopping in Swansea. She 'ave come back with a load of bargains, like a litre of vodka for £1.36. I asked her, "Where did you get all these goodies and at such a reasonable price?" "Oh Mam," she says to me, "they're just a few things that I've picked up here and there."

Cadwalider 'ave got the gripes, 'umming he is. I told our Shantelll not to feed him all that curry that was left over from last night.

Philll looks knackerated mind. I told him that he should take it easy and slip into something comfortable.

I've bought our Shantelll a little pressy, a mingy disc player. She loved it and she's walking round everywhere with headphones on. She looks awful important.

Tuesday

Rex next door is adamant that he's going to marry Elsie. I can't see it working, he's wearing her out now. He just don't stop and he loves her. She've had a historectomy. I said to her, "How do you manage love?" She said, "The nursery has gone, but the playroom is still there." I'll never understand that woman.

Paco is borrowing Shantelll's new car, the one with a lid.

She wasn't very happy with that idea. She loves her car more than him I think. She told him that the car was low on juice and to fill it up, so he gets 20 jiff lemons from the Co-op and shoved it in the car. It seemed to chug a bit. Pity, he can't help being from Spain, a third world country, no carpets and all that.

We need a couple of bob to go on 'oliday so Dai is poring bleach all over the carpets in the parlour and the dining room. Netty is well insured. Shantelll is going to say that there was a hole in the bottle and it spilled out of the shopping bag and on to the carpet. They wouldn't dare question us, living in a fine place like this. We look like money people. Roll on Benidorm.

Wednesday

The insurance man called and inspected the damaged carpets. "Not a problem Mrs Jenkins," he said, "and what a fine house you 'ave. I was just talking to your son Philll, he told me how you all came into money. I didn't know he's worked in Australia." "Oh really?" I says to him. "Yes," he said. "He told me that most of his work was down under."

Anyway, the blokie agreed on a price and I'm as happy as Larry. Wait till Netty sees the carpet. Shantelll is going to say that the baby spilled his milk everywhere.

Dai really misses the club. I think we are going to run a trip to the club at some point. It's so handy there. I mean to say, Elsie pops in there to get her slimming tablets and fish for the weekend.

Thursday

Philll 'ave decided to become a limited company, after all there's only so much you can take in there. Shantelll is going to be a director of the company, just to keep an eye on Philll and the business. After all, I don't want him to turn out to be a sucker. Shantelll will tell him what goes where. He's now got a fag machine installed in the new surgery, it's for when clients 'ave finished their treatment. Strange, they all seem to want a fag at the end of it all.

A blokie pulled up the other day in a right posh car and asked for our Philll, so I showed him to the surgery waiting room. He looked so eager to 'ave treatment, he must 'ave been in agony, love him.

Friday

Shantelll went to a new bank to 'ave her Giro money, and the cashier said to her, "Good morning, madam." And she says back, "How did you know?"

She is doing a bit of shopping for me to save me traipsing and she always manages to get a bargain. I seem to miss them. Just the other day she had a couple of packs of cider and they were really cheap, but I keep telling her, "Use a carrier bag, not your coat. It'll ruin the lining."

Shantelll

On the Gower
* WEEK 7 *

HIYA MY LOVELIES, IT'S GLADYS here with the 'appenings in our lovely lives here in the Mumbles, mind you I do miss Ponty Pantin. We're all taking a trip up to see Id and his nutty wife Netty this week.

Philll 'ave moved in to the penthouse apartment in sin city bay. He must 'ave seen it advertised in that penthouse magazine in his waiting room.

Shantelll has now got a bank account. The bank manager is taking her out this week for lunch. There's posh for ew. Like we always says, owt for a bit of dinner. Anyway, here goes...

Saturday

We're all down Philll's new apartment in sin city bay. The seagulls are rampant. He 'ave had new mirrors on the ceiling and a new bed with a hole to put your face through. At least I think that's what you put through. He 'ave got an intercom for the people with bad backs to ring outside, you 'ave to be careful, just in case you 'ave them Jerimiah Witnesess trying to get treatment on the sly.

I sent Dai out to get some Flash. Philll is so particular about his bathroom. Anyway, while Dai was out, he was walking up this back street and a lady said to him, "'ave you got a fiver for a short time?" Dai said to her, "I 'aven't had a fiver for a long time love."

He did eventually get back with the Flash, but he looked hot and bothered. Philll said to him about the lady, "Did you take her name? She might be encroaching on my territory." You can't trust anyone these days, can you?

We went back to the Mumbles about 8 that night, knackerarted. Fifteen rooms to clean in this mansion. I wish

I had someone to shine my taps for me.

Sunday

Shantelll is all geared up for lunch tomorrow with the new bank manager. She's got her new mini skirt all ready pressed. Dai said he thought it was for her Barbie doll. He said to her, "You'll never cover your private parts with that." Shantelll said, "Good, I'm trying to get an overdraft."

We had a lovely dinner down the Mumbles: cod and chips with baked beans over the top. Lush.

Philll came in the house and asked our Shantelll, "When's Mother's Day?" Shantelll said, "Nine months after Father's Day love." She's always been good with dates. Her Spanish husband Paco wants her to go upstairs for a siesta, but she told him straight, "It's a Vauxhall or nothing."

Monday

Shantelll is ready for the off. She's out with the bank manager today for a bit of grub. I wish Dai would go on a diet, but when he does, he gets trouble with his feet. He says they always end up in the chip shop.

Anyway, Shantelll had a lovely meeting with the new young bank manager. He told her about her savings account. He said, "It'll be long, hard and there'll be no withdrawals." She seemed quite happy about that. She told him, "I won't take it out, otherwise I might lose interest."

Dai's sister Slab is coming down to the mansion soon to 'ave a nose. It's no wonder her husband left her. If he was expecting a dreamboat, he got a tugboat instead.

Dai was feeding next door's pigeons to the cat when there was a knock on the front door. It was Slab, she said she was starving. I thought, you'll 'ave to bite your lip, there's nothing else here to eat. She had a good nose around and said, "Well, you've done well for yourself 'aven't you." I could see the green-eyed monster developing. People make me sick. You get a bit of luck and they're ready straight away to knock you down. If she thinks she's moving in here she can think again. If you remember, her husband ran off with another man. God, he had a narrow escape. He did 'ave a good job in decorating, he's now a passage designer in Cardiff.

We're off to see Id and Netty later. Shantelll is taking us up there in the new car she 'ave had from her nursing wages.

Anyway, we arrived at Ponty Pantin in the afternoon. I think we called at an inconvenient time because as we went through the door Idwal said to Netty, "I can feel you undressing me." Oh, he's a boy mind.

We've brought the ferret back up to Ponty Pantin, he won't settle down in the Mumbles, it's too posh for him. So we took the ferret in and Netty said, "Oh, is that Shantelll's baby? 'aven't he grown?" I've got to admit she's right around the twist. She thanked us for looking after the mansion and gave Shantelll £1,000 for her to 'ave the baby shaved. She's got a heart of gold mind.

Tuesday

Back in the mansion and Philll 'phoned for Shantelll. He wanted her to come down to sin city bay where she had a client, some big butch blokie, waiting for her. So I says to our Philll, "She's still in bed, can't you deal with him?" He said to me, "No Mam, he needs chest treatment, not back treatment." So I says back to him, "Try him with a bit of Vic love, that usually does the trick for your dad," but he seemed doubtful.

Philll wants to send a birthday present to that Chris Needs on the Radio Wales, so he's bought him a whole salami, that should keep him going for the weekend. Love him and his bad elbow as well. I told our Philll perhaps he'd be better offering him some treatment for his ailment, but he disagreed and said, "Mam, it's nice to 'ave something to open and 'ave something to nibble on in the long winter nights."

Wednesday

Our Philll is so busy he looks like an army of men 'ave run over him. Love him.

We had a 'phone call from Netty about the ferret, she thinks it's Shantelll's baby and she wants to know what milk to give it. So I told her to give him a some of the Co-op's finest in a dish on the floor, he'll manage OK. Honestly, I can't cope with all this.

Dai 'ave had some words with his sister. She's fishing for information on her husband, that one that run off with another fella. Philll said he knows him, how I don't know. I'm glad our Philll is normal and tidy. I couldn't stand all that nonsense in my house. I wish he'd hurry up and find a tidy little valleys girl.

Thursday

Duw the weather we get here, they ought to pay us to stay here and give us free heating and more black bags. I mean to say, when we 'ave visitors coming over from foreign parts the first thing I say is, "Fetch us a couple of cartons of fags will you?" Well, I mean to say, it's not right is it? They are made here, they should be cheaper here.

Shantelll said she wants to stand for parliament representing the Ponty Party, and she's going about canvassing for herself. She'd like to reduce the tax on fags and booze and ban VAT on gravestones and on adult clothes as well. Well, I means to say, you can't call clothes a luxury, can you? If you were to walk out in public with no clothes on you'd be arrested wouldn't you? She seems to 'ave had quite a few people in favour of her new ideas, especially that new bank manager. He said he'd like to be behind her all the way.

Friday

I'd love to see Shantelll as prime minister, she'd do a lot of good I think. Anyway, we're having a night in tonight in the mansion and we're all sitting around this massive table that we've got here and we've got posh wine from the continent that Malcolm the taxis got us. So we're having chips and corned beef hash with mushy peas. Dai will be blowing the bedclothes off again tonight.

On the Gower
* WEEK 8 *

WELL HIYA LOVES, how are you this week then? Shantelll has got to go to the doctor, something to do with her Mary Jones, and Dai 'ave gone completely ga ga, he's taken up line dancing and has got the full regalia – cowboy hat, the lot. Anyway, here goes...

Saturday

I've sent out Shantelll down the Co-op to get some of those orgasmic eggs, they're supposed to be better for you, mind you I always says they all come out of the same place, down below mind.

Our Dai 'ave just come though the door, he 'ave been to the opticians and he looks a bit worried, apparently the optician told him he'd 'ave to 'ave a pair of bisexuals. I told him straight, "Don't go bringing no flussies home here."

Shantelll 'ave nipped her new car down to a mate of Malcolm's to 'ave it serviced and he never charged her. I think she must 'ave smiled at him, she's got a lovely smile mind.

Dai's brother Willy 'ave just popped in with some stuff to shift: 100 mobile 'phones. I said to him, "Oh Willy, I'd love one of those." He said to me, "Take one Glad." He's as good as gold. So there's me with a funny 'phone. Mind you it's a natty little thing mind. The next time I'm in town or down sin city I'm gonna pose with my new 'phone, so there.

Sunday

I was in the shopping centre holding my new mobile 'phone, pretending that there's someone on the line, but as luck would 'ave it, there was me chatting away to nobody and everyone was looking, when the damn thing rang. Oh I felt a fool.

We've got a tidy dinner today: stuffed hearts and chips. They don't know class down here in the Mumbles let me tell you.

Our Shantelll is determined to get herself into politics, she's started a new party now called the Ponty Pantin Practical Party, it's all geared to the working man, she says. Cheaper fags and booze to start with.

She's off to the doctor's tomorrow, she's got a bad stomach, love her.

Monday

Shantelll has gone to the health centre to see the new posh doctor for a check up. He told her that she was a pregmatic girl and she asked him by how many months. She's a real good mother I 'ave to admit. The baby Cadwalider is nearly a year old now, he 'ave got all the latest tattoos and six studs in his ears and the best quality biker's jacket that money can buy.

We've invested in a motorised baby car for Cadwalider and he loves it. He nearly ran Idwal over the other week. Shantelll takes him up the waste ground by the river so he can go like hell in it as he's not 17 yet.

Our Shantelll met an old school friend the other day while she was coming back from the Co-op. Linda her name is, but they used to call her Loopy Loo in school because she couldn't say her tables off by heart. Mind you our Philll was clever in school, the teacher asked one little boy to stand up and say the 2 times table so he started, "1 times 2 is 2, 2 times 2 is 4..." all the way through. Then a little girl stood up and said the 3 times table, "1 times 3 is 3, 2 times 3 is 6..." right the way through. Then the teacher said to our Philll, "Philllip say the 9 times table." So he went, "Ug, ug, ug, ug, ug; ug, ug, ug, ug, ug..." Then he said to her, "I've forgotten the words, but I remember the tune, Miss."

Shantelll had sex education lessons in school and by the end of the term she was taking the class. She's very quick picking up things you know.

Philll used to be good at sport in school but he always fell in the mud and he likes to keep clean. The teacher said she couldn't get him out of the showers.

Our Maxine Roxanne is doing well in school, they are teaching her nutrition, the best things to eat, and apparently she's not to eat too many things with sugar in them. But like mother like daughter, she went behind the bike shed for a Twix.

Tuesday

I said to our Shantelll this morning, "You'll never guess what I found out the back of the house." And Shantelll says to me, "No, what?" I said back to her, "I found a contraceptive on top of the dustbin." Maxine Roxanne was listening by the door and she said to me, "Nana, what's a dustbin?" Well I mean to say, kids today, just what are they teaching them in school?

Shantelll went up the club with the baby to 'ave a couple of pints with the boys. She loves a game of bingo in the afternoon, she calls it afternoon delight and she marks 12 books. Duw she's clever, I told her to fetch me some fresh fish from the club and some cheap fags. Oh I do miss the club.

Wednesday

Shantelll 'ave been training little Cadwalider to 'ave a wee wee in the big toilet, anything to get him out of nappies, so she's put a box for him to stand on at the base of the big toilet and fair play mind, he's been doing well. One day he was stretching on tiptoes on the box to 'ave a wee wee and the lid came down on him. Bang it went and there was the poor little might holding himself down by there. He said to Shantelll, "Kiss it better Mammy." Shantelll said to him, "We'll 'ave none of your father's tricks here good boy."

Philll and Rapheal are planning to 'ave a special ceremony, they are going to be blessed. Well he 'ave always loved going to Sunday School, so good luck to them.

I'm glad to go to bed to be honest and I should sleep half-tidy tonight. Dai 'aven't had his usual curry, so we'll all 'ave a chance of some kip.

Thursday

Willy 'ave got rid of all them 'phones, Duw, he's a marvellous businessman mind. He can get anything you want. He got some fab balloons for our Maxine Roxanne's last birthday, 500 of them, so there we all were, pumping up the balloons ready for the party down the community centre and our Philll's pump broke. I told him straight, "Go and buy another one, otherwise you'll be out of poof, blowing all night." Shantelll just smiled and stuck her tongue out at him. "Leave him alone Mam," she said. "He's good at it."

Well, I can't believe it, my mobile 'phone 'ave rung. I was so excited, but it was only the 'phone company asking where I was. So I told them straight, "In the kitchen." Nosey lot. Well I mean to say, why do they want to know where I was with this 'phone? Willy said to me, "Say that you are in Nottingham." So I said, "I'm in Nottingham, born and bread and that's where I'll be if you want to see me." Then I said, "Prynhawn da," and switched the damn thing off.

Friday

Why does it always 'appen to me? The police 'ave been around, asking about mobile 'phones. They said there was a couple of hundred of them missing from a shop in Cardiff. You just wait till I see that Willy. He's so gullible, he's probably bought all them 'phones in good faith and hasn't realised that they've been nicked. Well I won't drop him in it, so I said to the policeman, "It was a present from Slab." Let them go and question her, all they'll get out of her is that her husband left her for another man. They'll soon get tired and drop it.

Our Philll 'ave had a lovely pink suit and the same again for Rapheal, They're off to get blessed in Swansea and of course, they've got Shantelll going with them. I think she's after some cigarettes 'cause I heard them saying something about a fag hag of honour. I hope that Philll will be alright down there in sin city. Rapheal is moving in with him, that'll keep him off the streets as they say and perhaps he won't find things so hard.

On the Gower
* WEEK 9 *

WELL HELLO MY LOVELIES. How are you this week? Shantelll has been canvassing to get herself in government, she's been doing really well. Lots of men seem to like her policies. Anyway here goes...

Saturday

Idwal 'ave had a bit of trouble with that Netty. She's 76 and wants a baby and nothing is putting her off. Mind you, she is knocking on a little and she hasn't left Idwal alone. She wants sex with him all the time. He's 88, I 'aven't got the heart to tell her it's not possible but Idwal keeps on trying like a good 'un. That's my boy!!!!!!!!!!

Shantelll, well she's been to visit the ear, nose and throat people down the hospital with the baby Cadwalider and she ended up talking to this doctor. I think he must be a bit lonely so our Shantelll said to this ear, nose and throat blokie, "If you are looking for love you are looking in the wrong places love." He examined Shantelll as well and said her chest wasn't bad. She told him straight, "All the men tell me that love." And off home they went.

Sunday

We went up the club for a change. I've got to admit, I do miss Ponty Pantin. The Mumbles is OK, but it hasn't got the class that we've got up here in the valleys.

Anyway, I was starving and the cockle man popped in the lounge bar so I thought to myself, I'll 'ave a bag of cockles, that will keep me going until I gets back to the Mumbles. So I says to him, "Give us a bag of cockles love." He said to me, "I 'aven't got any love. Sorry." So Shantelll said, "Ask him if he's got crabs Mam." So I says, "'ave you got crabs?" Boy, the look he gave me.

To be honest I was so glad to get back to our new home and we had a lovely Sunday dinner: chips and curry sauce. Lush.

Philll is booked right up this week, he've got clients in Ponty Pantin and down sin city bay and he've got them coming up here in the outhouse surgery outside the mansion. Shantelll reckons he don't know if he's Arthur or Martha. I told him straight, "Stick to Philll, it's a lovely little name."

Monday

Why does it always 'appen to me? The pipe 'ave burst in the bathroom and the water is flowing out everywhere. So Elsie gets some of Netty's new furs and drops them in the water, that should be a nice little claim for us, 'cause she don't know nothing what's going on. There's another 'oliday for us.

Netty wanted to know if our Philll was working for the council as a rent collector. She overheard Shantelll saying something about him being a rent boy.

I'm expecting the insurance man to call anytime soon. Those furs will never look the same again. I've made sure of that.

I've got to go up the chapel later on. I've offered to put flowers there as the lady that does them normally is off sick. She went to France for a weekend with the girls and she had a frog stuck in her throat. Duw, the French don't half eat some strange things, don't they.

Tuesday

Dai is getting really frisky lately. He walks to the dole office in Swansea. That's a good few miles I'm telling you.

Anyway, the insurance man called to see me and he wanted to know where I got the furs from and how much they were. I told him straight, "Do you expect me to ask my darling husband where he got the furs from and how much?" Some people 'ave got no class 'ave they? I told him my husband gave me these furs when we were on our yacht while visiting Gibraltar. He soon backed off when I said that. Anyway, with that Dai comes back from the dole office and says, "My feet are killing me in these shoes we had off the Social." I immediately jumped in and said, "That's the name of our yacht, the Social, because we throw so many parties in the summer while we're in the Med." Well, he seemed to chew that.

Wednesday

Went shopping with Shantelll. We went down the Strecher shop and then up to Markies. Shantelll calls them Strech Marks. We had some tidy food for the dogs, 9p a tin, but the labels had come off them, anyway, not to worry, I know what's in them.

A bit later on that day, Elsie comes in, moaning and groaning. She said, "That's the last time I eat mince from a tin. It's fresh for me from now on. I wouldn't give this to the dog, Gladys," she said. I didn't 'ave the heart to tell her.

Shantelll 'ave been having meeting with our Philll down in sin city, something about her nursing duties, mind you, she always looks a million dollars. She uses spray starch on her white uniform. Idwal asked her while she was ironing the other day, "What's that spray stuff you're using?" She told him it's to make her clothes stiff. Idwal wanted to borrow some, God, he's a funny one mind. I think he's a little bit sorry that he've married this American piece, she's a right handful. She's taking pregnancy tests everyday. God help us.

I cooked a fabluss tea for us: dripping and chips. Ooh lush. Dai always licks the plate clean, oh he's a pleasure to cook for.

Thursday

Philll has decided to send in a tape to Radio Wales, he wants to be a presenter. He'd like to do a chat show, something similar to Max Boyce's show but instead of calling it the *Final Curtain*, he's gonna call it the *Big End*. That should go down well.

Shantelll is still canvassing to get in power. I told her straight, as long as she can provide extra black sacks, she'll do for me. She'd make a great minister for social activities.

I miss my little jaunt up the club and I miss the free pineapple chunks I used to get. Oh Christopher the dog used to love them. Nobody can clean a toilet like me, you could eat your food off the floor when I used to do them. In fact, I remember about a year ago when we was living in Ponty Pantin, Freda from up the estate had her 50th birthday party up the club and she had so many people coming to the do, we put the buffet in the ladies. Oh, those were the days.

The ferret is back to normal now that he's back up Ponty Pantin but he's not fussed on that baby milk that Netty keeps giving him. God, she's round the twist. She said to Maxine Roxanne, "You look just like your cousin but with less hair."

Talking of Maxine Roxanne, she's got a little boyfriend and she must think the world of him. He's the local vicar's son and she keeps giving him her dinner money everyday. So I says to her, "Maxine Roxanne, why are you giving the little boy all your money?" She said, "Well Nan, I feels sorry for him. His dad only works one day a week."

Friday

I've got a tidy bit of cleaning to do here in the mansion and I've just been cleaning our Philll's room. Oh, he's a strange boy. He's always been jealous of our Shantell. He's always got to go one better. I found a load of old magazines in his cupboard with naked men in them. Anything Shantelll's got, he's got to 'ave the same. He's been like that since he was a youngster.

Anyway, the other day he was out down the local pub and the men in the bar were looking at a dirty calendar with naked ladies on it and apparently all the men were fancying these women. There was one picture of a naked lady sat on a stool and they showed it to Philll and our Philll said, "Oh damn, that's a lovely stool." He's always been into tidy furniture mind.

On the Gower

WELL HELLO MY LOVELIES. How are you this week? We're off on a boat trip round sin city bay this week and we're having a meal on it as well. Netty is still around the twist, she finds it very hard to consecrate. Anyway, here goes…

Saturday

Dai 'ave had a nat bite on his arm. I think it's from the dogs myself, 'umming they are, but it's a nasty little bite and Dai is quite upset about it. I always remember when we were in Spain and a mossceetoo bit our Shantelll, poor mossceetoo had to be taken to the Betty Ford clinic. Oh, she's a girl.

Philll is doing really well and Rapheal is always behind him like a tower of strength, a pillar, a guiding force, driving him in the right direction. Well you can't buy that these days can you, even though he's from a third world country with no carpets.

Netty thinks she's preggers at 76 and she's having morning sickness as well. I didn't know that Id had it still in him, or should I say out of him, as it were. Our old doctor is paying her a visit to check her over. He wants to look at her head not her Mary Jones.

We're leaving in a minute for the bay. We're going on a boat, can't wait. Our Shantelll loves seamen and they're so smart in their uniform.

We arrives at the boat place in the bay and on we goes. Philll was singing, "All the nice boys love a sailor," and Shantelll was singing, "There's a plaice for us." She loves a bit of fish. Dai was up on deck. He had to, the fags were upsetting too many people as usual. Duw, he looked like Leonardo Decapitated out there on the pointy bit of the ship. I'm glad to be honest that he's up on the deck, he's been letting off terrible lately.

Later on we goes for a meal, oh damn it was nice. Maxine Roxanne spewed all day, no change there. It's a pity she's so much like her mother.

We went back to the Mumbles that evening, Dai still letting off and Maxine Roxanne spewing everywhere. Aw it was a nice day. Well better out than in, innit?

Sunday

Dai is not going to chapel this morning. He's still doing the unsociables. I've got to make sure that he has a balanced diet, so I puts the potatoes on the bathroom scales, digital of course. Let's see if that will help him out and the rest of the household as well. As Dai says, "In church or chapel, let it rattle."

Simon, Philll's little friend, is coming up for dinner today. We're all having jumbo sausages and chips twice. I remember cutting up Philll's jumbo sausage when he was a little boy, ooh he didn't like it. He would say, "Mam, I'm not a money box." I never quite understood that.

Shantelll is so proud of her new sports car, the one with a lid. She took Idwal out the other day for a spin down the Mumbles Road and there he was, hair blowing in the wind and Shantelll running after it. Aw, she's a good girl mind.

We're all stopping in tonight to watch telly. Philll has bought us a dvd player. Dai can't get over it, a film on a coaster as he says, clever mind. Shantelll has bought her father a film: *Gone With the Wind*. He should 'ave starred in that.

Monday

The washing machine 'ave packed up and it's a new one. Netty bought all new when she bought the mansion. Well I'm not 'aving that, so the fella is coming round to fix it a little bit later on.

About 3 o'clock there's a knock on the door and there he is, the washing machine blokie. In he comes and the cheeky devil says to me, "What 'ave you been washing in this poor machine?" I told him straight, "There's nothing poor in this household my boy." Anyway, he pulls out a load of things from behind the drum, well it looks like the contents of a chemist shop. I'll kill that Philll. With that the washing machine man books in with our Philll and he said to me, "'ave this one on me misses." Well I couldn't argue could I?

Tuesday

Philll 'ave had more lubricant jelly delivered. Damn he must be using a lot of it. But his hair always looks nice I got to admit.

I 'ave to say it is really nice living down here in the Mumbles and if that Cathryn Zeta Jones does move here, she can come around with Mikie baby for chips, she'll enjoy that I'm sure. Elsie's making brawn and she does a lovely one. Now that would be a treat for the Douglas's's's's's.

Philll is doing extremely well, loads of money coming in. He do get up to some things mind you and he's always smiling, never down in the mouth. What I like is when you 'ave finished your treatment in his surgery, there's a jar of mints on the way out and some wet wipes. Aw he's so thoughtful. Mind you he's been in some tight jams in his time but I'm glad to say that he's coming good now. Aw, Mammy's little soldier.

Netty 'ave been buying baby clothes. How can anyone cope with all of this? Idwal must be a brave man. We've had the mansion valued, £3.2 million, so I says to the estate agent blokie, "How many thousands is that?" God he looked at me strange. Some people 'ave no sense do they.

Wednesday

A fella 'ave just come out from our Philll's surgery. He said his legs were like jelly. I asked if he'd like a seat, but he sharply refused. Aw he must 'ave piles or something. Mind you, piles always reminds me of Dai's brother Willy and his new girlfriend. They've moved to the north of Wales, something to do with business and he just had to move away, something to do with fresh air. Anyway, as I was saying, piles reminds me of them two: when they come down and go back up they're OK but when they come down and stay down, they're a pain in the butt.

Time for another exotic tea: chips and gravy. Delia eat your heart out girl! Yes, we love good food and you can't beat a night in with the catalogue, now that's what I call living butt.

Thursday

The washing machine bloke is back again. I thought to myself, that's strange, all the machinery seems to be working tidy like, but he went straight in to see our Philll again. There must be some tubes wanting unblocking somewhere I reckons. Philll never messes around: any trouble, get a man out to see to it. Philll 'ave always been a stickler for work, everything must be perfect and he's a hard worker, nothing's too much for him, the harder the better.

Friday

Simon is after a full-time job with our Philll, because Philll is starting a mobile bad back unit and Simon's been about. Philll's gonna call it Squeals on Wheels. He's such a clever boy mind and he's ordered a new van with dark windows in the back and front and he's had the sign writer to paint it as well. Damn it looks lush: 'Squeals on Wheels. Distance no object – we'll always come for you.'

All Change
* WEEK 1 *

WELL HELLO MY LOVELIES, it's Gladys again with the 'appenings that 'ave 'appened again this week here in the Mumbles and to be honest, you can stick it. What a tale I 'ave to tell this week, so here goes...

Saturday

That witch Netty 'ave had her memory back or something like that and she wants us out of the mansion because she's having a baby. Mind you, having a baby at 76! So down she came and she said, "How long 'ave you been squatting in my house?" Idwal tried to calm her down but there was no moving her. She wanted to 'ave her house back to 'ave her baby. Idwal said to me, "Don't worry, I've greased the stairs."

Anyway, she said that Philll could keep the outhouse with his surgery in it. She might want some treatment while she's preggers. That should prove interesting. Mind you, Philll thinks I'm daft. I know what's going on in that surgery on the side: he's selling fags on the knock. He must think I'm dim.

Anyway, we moves out and that Netty moves back in with Idwal. I'm glad mind, it's so nice to be back in Ponty Pantin. The people down there don't 'ave the class that we 'ave up here in the valleys. The ferret was glad to see us I must admit and he was so excited that he peed on Netty's new fur coat. Good enough, I thought. Shove that on your back, you miserable old goat.

Sunday

I've been cleaning like the clappers, the state she's left this house in is ridiculous. There's dust everywhere, the dirty old trollop that she is. Elsie is bunking on our sofa because

122

her council house is still rented out. They'll 'ave to go but Shantelll will see to that no problem.

Mind you Shantelll is disappointed at leaving Swansea. She loved walking along the beach at night collecting seashells but she always used to come back in with bites on her neck. I kept telling her to watch out for them mossceetoos. Love her little heart. Mind you she's a good little worker, she's done all the washing and drying for me.

So here we are again back in Ponty Pantin. I've just sat on the toilet, oh, it's lush to 'ave my fabluss wooden seat back, you can't beat it. And Philll is having his original surgery soundproofed. They don't half make a racket down there, the back is a delicate thing you know.

Monday

Out I goes to the Co-op with Shantelll of course, just to get a few little things in for our tea like, innit. I must remember to change the Giro book back to this address, otherwise we'll never 'ave another 'oliday this year.

With that, there's a knock on the door and there she is, Netty, all upset. I said to her, "What's the matter Nett?" She said to me, "I want to come back to Ponty Pantin. Idwal said that he could only rise to the occasion up here." So I thought to myself, what's the matter with all of them? So I sits her down and says to her, "Now Netty, where do you want to live, honestly?" She said, "Gladys, back here in the village."

So I phones Shantelll on her new mobile and tells her the news. Mind you, Netty gave me two grand for the trouble that she caused. The first thing that I'm gonna buy is a wooden seat for the bog in the mansion. So we hires a van again and moves back to the Mumbles. I wish it was a classier area like what I am used to.

I'm telling you now, that Idwal 'ave made a rod for his back. He must be going through hell. Anyway, we all arrives back in the mansion and Netty's only gone and left £500 for the milkman. Shantelll was landed and she's going out on the town tonight for a skinful.

Tuesday

I don't know where my priorities lie, I means to say that poor woman Netty thinks she's up the spout and I'll admit it's not for the lack of trying on Idwal's part. He's absolutely knackerated.

I'm sure Netty only wanted me to clean for her. I'm totally knackerated too and I've left all of my pineapple chunks back in Ponty Pantin, and the ferret, love him. Good job I didn't change the address for the Social. That might 'ave caused problems.

Shantelll said something about Guy Fawkes night, something about a banger up the M4. Strange girl, it's only April now.

Shantelll is doing a shift with Philll in the surgery and she said that she's putting her fee up. She said, "Well Mam, everything else goes up don't it?" Paco her husband is desperate to move back to Spain but Shantelll is adamant that she's staying here in Wales. She told him straight, "There's no Welsh schools in Spain, so that's that." She's ever so patriotic mind, she's even got a Welsh dragon on her knickers. She says it saves telling people where she's from.

Wednesday

Well what do you think about that Chris Needs? He's only gone and bought a new boat, so Shantelll popped down to Swansea to 'ave a peep at it. She said there were seamen everywhere and dressed smart too. She loves sailing as well you know, she likes the bobbing up and down I think. She's trying to coax Philll to 'ave one as well, God there'll be surgeries everywhere before long, but I suppose if the need is there, he's there to fill it.

Right, what about a bit of tea for our Dai? I looks in the fridge and thank God, Netty hadn't taken the dripping. Dai's favrite, especially the brown bit underneath. We certainly know how to live you know, only the best for my family. Dai has insisted on granary bread to put the dripping on, he's started to look after his health at long last.

Thursday

Idwal 'ave phoned here to say that Netty reckons she's in labour. It's probably wind. I'll send our Shantelll down with a baby's bonnet for her, that'll keep her happy for the moment.

Look out tonight, we're all going out for a slap up meal, steak and chips in Swansea, and then we're all off to the casino. We gets into this posh restaurant and we all has steak and chips. The waiter said to Dai, "Would sir like a napkin?" Dai said, "No butt, it's OK, we've got plenty of disposables with us. The baby's already done a womper before we left home, but thanks anyway. I'll take one or two just in case he has the gripes on the way home."

Then off we goes to the casino in Swansea and on the way in this fella in a bouncer's suit asked Dai if he'd like some chips. Dai told him straight, "No thanks butt, we've just had a cart load down the road."

Philll knew quite a few of the people there and they were all well to do, pity that they've all got bad backs mind. Shantelll sat on a table, you know the one, it's got a spin dryer built in to it. Well that's handy mind in case you don't 'ave time to go home and change, very considerate I call that. I'm so proud of my children. The croopy fella was speaking French to all the players and Shantelll and Philll seemed to understand the lot. Shantelll was given a load of Monopoly money by this rich looking fella and apparently he wanted to make another appointment with her. God love him, his back must be awful.

Friday

Woke up with a terrible hangover. The drinks kept coming all night and I must admit I sank a few pints of Dark. I've been up all night peeing. Philll said that he had a lot of business from there last night. He'll put them right. He's very good sorting out the men. He'll 'ave them up and about in a jiff.

Shantelll is still in bed and Paco's not speaking to her, mind you it doesn't matter, she doesn't understand him at the best of times with that accent and all.

I had a bit of a shock the other day, our Cadwalider said to me, "Hola abwela, como estass Mama?" I said to him, "Now look here Antonio Basteeria, you are Welsh, we'll 'ave none of that foreign talk here. Where do you think you are, Benidorm?" Mind you, Shantelll said when he's older he'll be handy to order drinks abroad if she quarrels with Paco. That's our Shantelll, upstairs for thinking, downstairs for miniskirts.

Well what a week this has been: moving in and out, Netty convinced she's preggers, casinos, posh restaurants, ferrets peeing everywhere; the next thing you know Philll will tell me he's found a nice little valleys girl and he'll want to get married. Do you know, it's no wonder I'm feeling queer.

All Change
* WEEK 2 *

WELL HELLO MY LOVELIES. It's Gladys here with the 'appenings that 'ave 'appened here in the Jenkins's's's's's family. As you know, last week we moved back to Ponty Pantin because of that miserable American piece and then we moved back to the Mumbles when she had a change of heart. Anyway here goes...

Saturday

Loads of washing to do. Thank goodness that the washing machine man 'ave serviced the machine the other day. He did a good job of it and then he went to see Philll for a service in the surgery. I'm thinking of going down to see Madam Yeoman to get some palms for the Easter bank 'oliday, they'll look fabs down here in the Mumbles and they'll block out the gas works across the water. That'll add money to this place, a good view is important.

Our Philll is taking it easy lately and he's got a bar installed in the surgery now. Oh you can't beat a mouthful of Gordon's, that's what he do say and Shantelll is partial to a Black Russian. Dai 'ave got his eye on our Philll's bar but he's too frightened to go in and pinch a drink. I told him straight, "C'mon Dai, you've seen it all before." But there was no moving him.

Idwal 'ave got his work cut out with that Netty. She believes that she's in labour. Well aren't we all love, at the end of the day?

We're going up the club tonight. There's a – yes you've guessed it – male stripper there: King Dong from Hong Kong he's called. But our Philll seems to know him from before. His real name is Malcolm from Merthyr. I'll let you know what 'appens tomorrow.

Sunday

I can't face going to chapel after last night. It wouldn't be right, oh it was frightening. As per usual Philll and Shantelll was in the front seats and this big massive blokie came out dressed as a fireman clutching a big hose pipe. He came up to Dai and Dai said to him, "Whose pipes that hose butt?" Philll set the ashtray on fire just to test him out and Shantelll climbed up a tree outside screaming for help. They had a good night. I was happy enough with the bingo, that's exciting enough for me, let me tell you.

Dinner time and I don't know what I'm to do. With all the fussing around yesterday I forgot to leave the tripe and hearts out of the freezer so it's fish fingers now. Our Philll said, "Oh Mam, I hates fish." Do you know there's no pleasing people is there? I'd like to see what he's got in his freezer down in his apartment in sin city bay. It'll never compare to Mam's cooking, no way.

Anyway, we all ate the grub and they're all happy now because I'm paying for a Chinese tonight.

Monday

Dai 'ave got the runs. He tried to eat a bit of the frozen chickling. I told him not to, he'll never learn. Anyway, the 'phone just went and it's Idwal on the line asking what to do because Netty reckons the baby is due. I told him straight, "It's all in her mind, it's probably wind, give her back a rub for a change." But there was no telling him, he wanted me up the house to see to her.

So me and our Shantelll goes up to them and there's Netty lying on the bed legs all positioned right to 'ave the baby. Shantelll asked, "Shall I boil some water Mam, just in case?" So I says, "Yes love, milk and two sugars."

I tried to tell Netty that it's not a baby she's having, but there was no telling her. So we had to pretend that she was giving birth and after about two hours, she gave a final shove and said, "There you are – what is it: a boy or a girl?" Shantelll, quick thinking mind, said, "A boy, Netty," and handed her the ferret. Oh she was landed.

I'm telling you now, things are getting more difficult around here by the minute.

Tuesday

We sent a card to Netty and her new baby as she thinks it is. She's naming the ferret Jason. I don't think he'll like that. All I want is a peaceful life.

Next thing there's a knock on the door and there's a blokie there full of tattoos looking for Dai's brother, Willy. I said to him, "Oh love he's living up in North Wales now, somewhere near Bangor." The fella seemed quite nice and left his name, Basher Williams. I told him the next time Willy 'phoned I'd pass on the message. Damn he was very polite and he had gorgeous tattoos, fair play mind.

We are thinking of having a party for the neighbours, there's a few big wigs living around here you know. We are going to ask the mayor of Ponty Pantin to come along, and of course Bonnie Tyler and maybe even Cath Zeta Douglas, she seems like a nice girl. Philll is seeing to the food and Shantelll is going to be mine host. This will take a fair bit of planning but we'll do it. We'll 'ave the party next week sometime. I wonder if that Chris Needs will come along? They reckon he'll push in anywhere. Elsie's already excited, she's on the brawn making trail as we speak. You can't beat a bit of brawn.

Wednesday

Well I can't wait for next week. I'm only wondering, should we ask some of the Assembly Members to come along? I reckon we should keep in with the councillors too, at arm's length mind. You never know, we might need some extra black bags in the future.

We're off to Makkros today to get a few things for the party next week. We needs cocktail sticks for the sausages and Philll told me to get napkins for the guests to wipe their faces and hands when they were eating food, but I can't see that being any good. I don't fancy wiping my face in a pamper. I'll get some kitchen roll. Cath Zet won't mind. It'll be home from home for her. Marvellous.

The dog food was cheap mind you so we got a few slabs of that and we had two new wide screen tellys, just to show off when the guests arrive.

Shantelll was given a load of perfume samples, well she reckons they were samples, but they were big massive bottles. I think the chap who worked on the perfume counter owed her a favour or two. I heard him saying to our Shantelll, "You won't say nothing to my wife will you?" He can't be taking perfume home to his wife I reckons. I suppose his wife would be jealous if she found out that Shantelll had a load off him.

Thursday

Well we've sent out the invitations to the guests. Shantelll 'ave sent her quota to a taxi man in town, the perfume rep up Makkros, the head of traffic wardens and three brick layers on the council.

Philll 'ave sent invitations to Dale Winton, Julian Clary, Chris Needs, three male strippers and that new fella that 'ave just moved into Ponty Pantin, the one with the new Austrian blinds and a pink beetle car. Mind you, I thinks to myself, that new boy makes a lovely queesh. Handy to know I reckons.

Dai 'ave invited Malcolm the taxis, Cledwyn from the club and Mansell the drain cleaner. Duw, you want to see what he pulls out of a drain, it was like jam it was the other day. How he does it I'll never know, and he eats his sandwiches at the same time.

I really do think that the guests are going to be so interesting and a good mix of people. I can't wait for next week. Mind you, Netty's bringing the baby – the ferret that is – down to the party, perhaps we should invite Rolf Harris along, he's good with animals ain't he?

Friday

A letter 'ave come today to the mansion here in the Mumbles asking us for council tax. Is there something wrong with them? They know that Dai 'ave got an incurable bad back, anyone can see that, and Shantelll is a single mother. We don't show Paco to anyone, we said that he was an exchange student. Idwal is the owner as far as the council is concerned, so there should be nothing to pay.

They'll know it if I gets myself down them council offices let me tell you. If people think they can take us for a ride they've got another think coming.

Philll 'ave had a new machine fitted to the surgery toilet wall, it's a chewing gum machine. I'm telling you now, it'll never take off. They tastes like rubber but there is a hint of strawberry. Uch y fi! Never in Europe.

Jason

All Change
* WEEK 3 *

WELL HELLO MY LOVELIES, it's Gladys here again with the doings that 'ave been done here in our wonderful family, the Jenkins's's's's's. I hope you are all well. Here goes...

Saturday

The plans are all on for our party on Friday and I've got to nip in to Swansea to get a few Easter eggs for the family.

I bought our Shantelll a lovely egg, with Easter bunnies all over it. Well, Paco always 'ave told her she's like a bunny. I've bought our Philll a special Easter treat because he's turned vegetarian lately, so I've bought him a fondant chicken. He always liked a bit of meat, but he must be on the turn. Strange boy. Idwal 'ave had white chocolate drops and we've bought that Netty a book on how to look after a ferret, seeing that she thinks that the ferret is her child. She's still around the twist.

That Philll don't stop working in that surgery, love him. He've had it hard lately what with the tax man and the vat man and a few business people he've been seeing to.

Shantelll is going into Swansea for an audition to model for a catalogue. She'll do well – she'll do anything to take her clothes off. I'll let you know what 'appens.

The party is next Friday, I hope we get all the bits and bobs done in time. I've called directory enquiries to find out Cathryn Zeta Jones' 'phone number but they won't give it to me. I told them we're almost neighbours, so the woman said, "Why don't you nip in and see her?" I might just do that.

Sunday

I'm off to chapel today to put a word in upstairs with Himself to let us win the lottery, and to see that Mrs Evans from Ponty

Pantin, she still owes me catalogue money. Some people just take and take don't they? Got to chapel, no sign of her. I'll nab her in the bingo.

We've got a fab Sunday dinner today: boil in the bag beef and gravy from the Co-op over chips. Lush. Dai always manages to get gravy down his front, so I told him to change his shirt but he wouldn't 'ave it. He said it was his dinner jacket, you can see the dinner down the front of it. He's not from the same valley as me, my valley is much classier than his, no names mentioned mind.

Talking of valleys, Philll 'ave got a new dvd for tonight, it's called *The Life Story of the Village People*. It'll probably be a load of men venturing into holes looking dirty. I thought I'd seen it all before on the BBC but until I saw his film, I never realised that miners wore feathers and cowboy hats. You learn something new every day don't you?

Monday

Shantelll 'ave had the job posing on the catalogue and her first assignment is lingerie. I told her to keep her hand on her tuppence but she said to me, "Don't worry Mam, the job pays more than that." So I'm stuck with Cadwalider now everyday while she takes her clothes off. She should get used to it before long. Paco is pretty good with the baby and he speaks Spanish to him all of the time and the baby says back, "What's he saying Nan?" Oh, he's picking up Spanish tidy now.

The food is all done and is in the freezer ready to be defrosted. We've frozen everything: sandwiches, milk, sausage rolls and even the serviettes. Nothing can go wrong now, I'm telling you.

Mind you, I'm a little worried. Cath Zet 'aven't written back to tell us that they are coming. I hope they turn up, that'll be a real talking point for the neighbours.

I've frozen Elsie's brawn as well, wait till Michael Douglas tastes that, he'll love it here in Wales, let me tell you now. The Americans don't 'ave such nice food as us do they? They only 'aves burgers and chips and stuff. They love coming her for a bit of culture.

Tuesday

Shantelll 'ave done well with her modelling and she's had cards printed saying: 'Beautiful female model, specialising in knickers and the nuddy.' She's gonna go places that one. You know, she's also been offered a job lap dancing, she said she'd be swinging round a pole. God help him, that's what I do say.

We've had a few answers from our guests. There's a few flussies coming along, friends of Philll, and there's a few of Dai's butties coming down here from the club. The Douglas's's's's's will be thrilled to meet such lovely folk. I hope that Bonnie Tyler comes, she can sing my favrite song for me: 'It's a Hard Egg'. That's a good one that and her husband is so nice as well.

Netty 'ave got the ferret dressed in a diaper and a bonnet and is pushing him around in a pram. Mind you, the people in Ponty Pantin are really good, they'll play along with her just to keep Idwal happy. The only thing I'm worried about is that she wants to 'ave the ferret baptised. The ferret hates water, there'll be uproar. I'm dreading that.

Wednesday

Still no news from the Douglas's's's's's, we'll see what 'appens, mind you we're not short of celebrities. We've got the stripper coming – King Dong from Hong Kong – and two pole dancers, friends of Shantelll. Well I mean to say, if them dancers can come from Poland, surely Bonnie and Cathryn can pop in from Swansea, can't they?

Cadwalider 'ave spewed everywhere. I think the beer doesn't agree with him. I told our Dai not to put beer in his bottle but Dai keeps on insisting that if it was good enough for him it's good enough for Caddy bach.

Maxine Roxanne loves a vodka in her milkshake ever since Shantelll put it in by mistake a couple of years ago. Mind you, she's doing well in school, she knows all about sex education and family planning. She told me the other day about different forms of contradiction. She said, "There's a balloon you can use Nan, or a tablet, or if all else fails, tie a knot in it." She's so clever, love her.

Thursday

I've started to lay out the table: serviettes and things and the dishes and forks and stuff, and if I run out of serviettes I've got a catering pack of kitchen roll from Makkros. Mind you, we still do a lot of shopping in Asda's. I see that Chris Needs there quite often, arguing with the bacon slicer blokie. I've got a load of diet drinks in case there's a few diabolics there, you never know do you, and sweeteners of course, they will 'ave pride of place in the centre of the table.

A fella 'ave just called to see our Philll. I think to be honest Philll 'ave forgotten about him, he's so busy, he's got customers popping in from everywhere. He's recently been to the dentist to 'ave his teeth seen to, apparently his teeth were too sharp and he had to 'ave them rounded off, he must be cutting his lip or something. You 'ave to be careful don't you? Anyway this fella that called for our Philll, I told him, "Don't worry, Philll will slip you in as soon as he's finished his last patient. Put your handbag down by here my love, I'll keep an eye on it for you." He seemed very grateful, love him. And as sure as anything, out came our Philll and said, "Sorry to keep you waiting, the last patient came late."

Well the big day is tomorrow and I hope it's a success. I really want the big wigs around here in the Mumbles to get to know us. God knows, this place needs a bit of class injected into it. The strange thing is that nobody here walks in the house and shouts, they all knocks the door instead.

I always remember once, back in Ponty Pantin, Dai was in the house on his own and he was on the toilet and the minister called in to see us. He shouted, "Anyone at home?" Dai said, "Hang on a minute Vic, I've got my hands full. Can you leave some toilet paper outside the toilet door for me?" And love him, he did as well. Now you don't get that in the big cities do you?

Philll's patient has just come out of the surgery and he looks pleased as punch. I said to him, "Is your back better love?" He said, "Oh yes, and my front." I thought to myself, I didn't know that our Philll was seeing to chest complaints as well. What a talented boy I 'ave.

Friday

Well the big day has arrived and the food looks wonderful: potato salad, coleslaw, bread and gravy dripping and cockles. Oh, the stars will love all of this. Anyway, 7 o'clock, there's a few here: the stripper, some of Philll's friends, Shantelll's gentleman friends from the council, a couple of labourers, butties of Dai, and Netty and the ferret in a bonnet. I'm hoping that that weather blokie Derek Brockerly and that Mal Pope might turn up. Philll's got his eye on him. I think he wants Mal to show him the ropes about radio.

The food has disappeared and we've had quite a few people in and out, even that new woman with the shaved head and Doctor Martin boots 'ave called in. Oh, I like that Les a lot.

Philll and Shantelll 'ave done us proud. They've had a kissagram for Dai, a policewoman showing all her bra and knickers and boy was she a well-blessed girl. Our Dai's eyes lit up like a match and she sat on his lap and our Dai said, "You'll never fall on your face my good girl."

Mind you that party went all right and everyone seemed to enjoy it. It's pity that the Douglas's's's's's didn't turn up. Never mind, maybe next year.

Rapheal has taken Philll upstairs by the hand, aw love him, these Spanish boys must 'ave terrible bad backs, must be all that sun they get on them, but fear not Philll will put him right – he carries his talents with him everywhere he goes. I hope Rapheal feels better after some treatment from Philll. I suppose it's only a shot in the dark after all.

All Change
* WEEK 4 *

WELL HELLO MY LOVELIES. How are you again? I hope you've had a lush week. We had a lovely party last week, it was a great success. People here in the Mumbles seem to like us very much. It's about time they had a bit of class here. Anyway here goes…

Saturday

What a mess after that do last night. Never mind, our Shantelll is cleaning up like the clappers. It keeps her in trim for her modelling work.

Our Philll met up with an East German in the party, mind you, God knows how he got there. Philll said to him, "I'm not fussed on the east, I'd rather go south myself, it's warmer and more interesting." He's always been good at geography mind.

There's a nice piece of brawn left and Dai has nabbed it for his tea. Duw, he's a boy mind, he never misses a trick. That poor Idwal is still having to put up with Miss America 1920, how he does it I'll never know.

Sunday

Shantelll is preparing clothes ready for her modelling engagement tomorrow. She's a right good looker, she's modelling knickers for a catalogue. She said to me, "Mam 'ave you got a razor?" I told her straight, "Don't be silly our Shantelll, nobody is going to look under your arms when you are modelling knickers." She'll never learn, silly girl. She said to me, "No Mam, it's for my Mary Jones." I told her straight, "Tell Mary Jones to buy her own razor."

The next thing there's a knock on the door. It was the Outland Revenue, they wanted to know if we were running a business here. I told them straight, "No way. Our Philll works voluntary helping the community with their bad backs. He should really 'ave an OBE like that Iris Williams do 'ave." They didn't seem convinced. So out comes the Welsh cakes and we sat in the main kitchen of the mansion with Netty's best Royal Albert china. I told them straight, "We're a poor family and we don't 'ave much, just these simple surroundings." Do you know it's not fair, we pay tax on wages and on fags and then they still want to charge tax on other things that are important in life, like perfumes, pantie girdles and diet cola. I told them straight, "It's not good enough." Just then Philll walked into the room and one of the blokies seemed to know him. They had a quick chat in the other room and after that everything was sorted. That's my boy. I thought I'd seen him somewhere before.

Just then Shantelll walked into the room in her new bask that she was modelling and said, "Mam, can you see Mary Jones. Does she look alright?" I thought to myself, what does she want to change her name for now? Shantelll with three lll's is a lovely name. The Outland Revenue soon left.

Monday

Shantelll has left for work. It's all cash in hand, marvellous mind, and damn she looks fabs in her new sports car. She's now claiming housing benefit for staying in her bedroom. She's got it down as bed and breakfast with use of washing machine. She's not dull you know. She made about two grand last week and there's nothing anyone can do about it. I've always said she's sitting on a fortune, you know.

The people 'ave moved out of Elsie's in Ponty Pantin and she's moving back in with Rex, her toy boy. She prefers it back in the village, she misses the graffiti, there's not much down here in the big city, not like back home. I'm glad to be honest, she's always moaning about that 18 year old: he's always after her for a bit of nonsense. The other day he started his antics again in Asda's, right by the frozen food. I told her straight, "Don't let any man come between you and your chicken dippers girl. You'll be sorry."

Tuesday

Idwal has got to go and renew his disabled sticker for the car. He's trying for half a dozen – one for each car. I hope he gets them. We're always forgetting them when we go out. Mind you, it's awful handy to 'ave the sticker. The other day Shantelll parked outside the police station and we walked half a mile to the supermarket. Duw, it's nice to be in control isn't it? Ha ha!

Anyway, back comes our Shantelll from work and she was complaining like hell. The tassels they gave her were very uncomfortable. I told her straight, "Don't bother modelling cushions, stick to what you are good at."

With that the surgery door opened and out comes this gorgeous young man and our Philll says to him, "I hope you come again." Oh he's awful polite mind. I always says, us Welsh always keeps a welcome in the hillside. Do you know why? 'Cause we don't want anyone in our houses, that's why.

We had a lovely tea, goodness knows our Philll and Shantelll 'ave to keep their strength up. Mind you, Philll won't eat beans, he reckons wind could ruin his business.

Wednesday

Maxine Roxanne 'ave got a new little boyfriend, so I says to her, "How's your little boyfriend?" She says to me, "Frisky Nan, frisky." Aw she's following our Shantelll exactly. Keep 'em sweet and then pinch their dinner money. That's my girl.

Dai 'ave washed his one and only suit, but he 'ave put it in the dish washer by mistake. It 'ave shrunk, but it shines lovely mind. I'll 'ave to see about having a piece put in the back of the trousers so he can wear them again. Silly man.

Thursday

We're trying desperate like to teach Paco and Rapheal to speak English tidy, like what we do do and to be honest they've picked up the essentials quite tidy. Like, 'Where's my Giro to then butt?' and, 'I need a decorating grant, love.' That's the trouble, you never get the important things to say in a phrase book do you? Just stupid things like: 'I left my teeth in a cup by the bed in my hotel room.' I mean to say, how far will you get with all of that?

You need to be in the country to learn proper tidy like. Elsie 'ave taught that Rex to say: 'I need dental treatment. I must 'ave six gold teeth please'. Oh yes, always say please. I've brought my kids up half tidy, I 'ave always told them to say please and thank you and always tell them: "You're not working, just helping out voluntary like, innit?"

Philll is going to contact that Chris Needs to see if he'll pop our Shantelll over to Jersey on his boat on a fag run. I've heard that that Chris likes a fag now and again, there could be a nice little earner there.

Friday

Well another week 'ave gone and I'm still no better off, still waiting to hear about our increase with the Giro and we are still waiting to hear about the housing benefit. We told the council that we had to live in a big house as Idwal and Shantelll 'ave got claustrophobia and they've tried to get over it as best they can, but the cream just doesn't work. Netty has put the ferret's name down to go to the Welsh school. Well as long as it keeps her happy, that'll do me.

Paco, that's Shantelll's Spanish husband, 'ave just had a copy of the new catalogue that Shantelll is modelling in. Mind you, I've never heard of this catalogue before. It's called *Slag Heap*, but there you are, standards 'ave all gone out through the door today.

Anyway, that's about it for this week. I hope we hear from the Social soon – we fancy a trip to the Caribbean. I'll let you know next week.

WELL HELLO MY LOVELIES, how are you this week? Things are going well here in the Mumbles, we 'ave definitely brought a bit of class to the area – not a moment too soon, I hastens to add.

Elsie is having a bit of trouble with her Spanish toy boy Rex. I'll tell you more about that later on. Here goes...

All Change
* WEEK 5 *

WELL HELLO MY LOVELIES, how are you this week? Things are going well here in the Mumbles, we 'ave definitely brought a bit of class to the area – not a moment too soon, I hastens to add.

Elsie is having a bit of trouble with her Spanish toy boy Rex. I'll tell you more about that later on. Here goes…

Saturday

A fella came to the door selling birds in a cage, pretty they were as well. I shouted up the stairs to our Philll, "Do you fancy a couple of birds love?" He said, "No Mam, I'm not really into them to be honest." But you know me. I felt so sorry for them, so I took two in a cage. I couldn't let them go to a bad home.

We've named the birds Timmy and Tommy, two boys they are and Philll approved of that. He's no good with the girls, they always want to pinch his handbag. God, he's so smart mind. Shantelll is always asking to borrow his clothes, just the other day she borrowed a pair of his fishnet stockings. He's got a heart of gold mind

Elsie is having a bit of a time with that Rex. He wants a child but Elsie keeps on telling him the nursery has gone but the playroom is still there. He'll never learn.

Dai 'ave had an increase in his Giro this week, a clothes grant. About time as well. Shantelll is taking him down to the £1 shop to look for pants and vests.

Netty is teaching the ferret to speak some Welsh phrases she's learned off our Shantelll, like: 'I love you, Pres-dat-in' and 'Take her up the mountain to Bangor.' Oh, Shantelll had top marks in Welsh in school.

Sunday

There's a new market just opened today in Ponty Pantin and we're off for a gander. Anyway we gets up there and there's loads of stalls. We went to the first one and they had beautiful veg and the man gave our Shantelll a bag of fruit for nothing. He said that he'd call to see her one day. He must be wanting some Welsh lessons. Then we went to a clothes stall and there was this lovely looking young man selling his wears. Philll had a massive discount with him. They all seemed to know Philll and Shantelll.

Then we went to the local cafe and the man behind the counter said, "I've got a certificate for my food." Shantelll said, "Yes and I've had a few days off work too since I've been eating here." Anyway, we all had pie and chips with gravy. We know how to live let me tell you.

Do you know that our Philll wanted to go to chapel today. He said he fancied a few hymns: "Him, him and him." Our Shantelll said, "Oh he's so musical. I'd love to see him playing the organ."

Monday

Philll is hard at it down in the surgery and he's taken a bit extra hair gel with him. It don't half stiffen his hair. I could hear a load of moans and groans coming from the surgery, how he puts up with it I'll never know.

He's playing some tune down there. I think it's by Donna Summer: 'Love to love you baby.' Pretty little tune. Mind, he wants to open those curtains for a bit of light and I'm worried about his accounts: if he's not careful he'll find himself in a dark hole.

Shantelll is seeing to the books for the surgery business. I heard her the other day, "One for Mr Brown, seven for me." Damn she's a clever girl, nobody will get one over on her.

Mind you our Shantelll has done well with her modelling too. She was modelling knickers last week in a new catalogue called *Slag Heap* and the manager wants her and Philll to go to Amsterdam to model out there. Shantelll seemed quite excited about the idea of it, she said she'd like to bring an under privileged youngster back with her. I told her straight, "Don't you bring no dope back here. Your father's dull enough."

Tuesday

Idwal 'ave had a gutsful of that American dame. She's putting years on him with this idea that the ferret is her child. She's completely round the twist. To be honest, I shouldn't say really but I will: Idwal is having an affair with another woman from up the council estate and she've had more knocks than our front door, let me tell you. The men are back and fore all times of day and night, but if it keeps our Idwal happy, who am I to put a stop to it.

Mind you I thought our Dai was carrying on a few years ago. He asked me for clean underpants so I told him, "What's wrong with the ones you've got on? They were clean week last Thursday." I told him straight, "Don't go mining in other caves or there'll be no toad in the hole here, right?"

Wednesday

Shantelll has renewed her passport, she is adamant she wants to go to Amsterdam to do this modelling contract. She said to me, "Mam, I'll do well, there's only a load of dykes out there." Her Spanish husband Paco doesn't mind a bit, he's all for it. I think he's just after some duty free when she gets back.

The birds are twittering like the clappers and they keep on kissing each other. I can't understand it, they're two boys and I'm telling you I'm having none of that in my house.

Philll slips off into the surgery, very quietly, he doesn't like me shouting at the birds. Mind you he's gone a little bit religious. He was reading a magazine the other day and at the end he said, "Ah men."

We had a lovely tea this evening: curry sauce and chips. It was a bit hot mind and Philll nearly choked. I told him straight, "Blow on them, that's my boy."

Thursday

Idwal is a worry to me. He's trying to please two women at the same time. I clouted our Dai when he offered to help him out but Idwal is coming back here absolutely knackered. This piece from up the council estate has been helping herself to his money. Apparently she nicked fifty quid off him while he was rinsing his teeth out. Our Shantelll went up there to sort her out and she had the money back. I think it was something to do with the DHSS. Shantelll has got something on her, a breeze block probably. Anyway, all's well that ends well. Idwal 'ave had his money back.

There's a knock on the door and there's a chap there from the hardware store and he gave our Shantelll a new kettle, two toasters and a dvd player. Silly girl, she must 'ave left them on the counter. She said to him, "See you again next week and give my regards to your wife." She's such a thoughtful girl mind.

Friday

Shantelll 'ave had stickers done, I think to be honest she's pinched them off the bus. They say: 'Pay as you enter'. I can't understand it, what does she want to drive a bus for? She's got a lovely little car outside the door mind and it goes up the mountain great in second gear and holds the road too, love it, never a skid mark in sight. Good road holding, that's what she's got.

Philll's mobile bad back unit is doing well, the one called Squeals on Wheels. He gets in the queerest of places, but where there's a will there's a way, that's what he always says. You can't keep a good man down!

Just the other day there was a delivery to the house. It said on it something like 'Summers toys' but I've said nothing to Philll that I've seen the box. I don't want to spoil the surprise. I bet it's a patio set for up the back. He thinks I'm dull but I know what's going on. I can see it all now: table and chairs and posh cushions to sit on. 'Summers toys', eh? I can't wait to try them out. I hope they'll fit.

All Change
* WEEK 6 *

WELL HELLO MY LOVELIES, how are you this week? Shantelll has done ever so well with her modelling and she's off to Amsterdam this week with Philll to do some more.

I'm so lucky to 'ave such a talented family and they're so rich as well. Anyway, here goes...

Saturday

There's all hell let loose in our house, or should I say Netty's mansion. There's leather trousers and g strings everywhere and that's just Philll. I wish I was 20 years younger, I'd go with them to Amsterdam. I'm making sure that they've got all their documents ready this time because last time Shantelll's passport was out of date. I don't want my two children on that telly programme *Airport* with that stingy fella, what's his name now? John Nettles.

They must be celebrating someone's birthday out there – Philll and our Shantelll 'ave filled their suit cases with balloons, but it's strange that they've chosen clear ones, not pink or blue. That party will go with a bang I'm telling you.

Dai 'ave warned our Philll not to come home without a load of fags. Shantelll said he'd never fit them all in his suitcase. I've put tubs of lava bread in for them as well, and a bit of oatmeal separate to sprinkle on top. Damn they'll enjoy that.

God I'm gonna miss them and they're only going for a few days. Mothers are silly billys aren't they? Anyway must press on, I 'aven't put the cockles in their cases yet.

Sunday

Malcolm the taxis is taking them down sin city airport this morning. I don't know what company they are flying with, but

145

I heard our Shantelll talking to Philll about an easy jump.

I hope those men trolley dollies don't distract our Philll while he's up there. I've warned him to pay attention to the safety details in case of an emergency. Someone is going to 'ave to take that boy firmly in hand, let me tell you.

Anyway, Malcolm arrives and puts the suitcases in the taxi and there's me on the door step crying and shouting to them not to get into any tight spots.

And it's back to normality for me, cooking Sunday dinner for this lot that's left. That Netty is coming down here to the Mumbles for dinner today, dear me. She's round the twist. She was looking at a post card of the station with Llanfair pwllgwyngyllgogeryllchwrndrwdwllllandisillogogogoch on it and she said, "Don't they 'ave small stations here?"

I can't cope anymore.

Monday

I had a 'phone call from our Shantelll from up 'olland and they've arrived tidy like. I told our Shantelll to look out for them dykes. Mind, I warned our Philll not to do what that little Dutch boy did, "Don't put your finger in a dyke, you'll get no thanks, it's not your country."

Apparently they are off to do some filming later on today, it's a public information film I think. Our Shantelll said it was called *Snakes in the Grass*. Well you can't be too careful can you? I'll let you know more from 'olland as we find out more.

Netty is still here in Swansea with us, hasn't she got a home to go to? The ferret is demented. It's got a school cap and a tie and a satchel and he looks up to me as if to say, "Why me Mam? Why me?"

Dai 'ave had a new pair of trousers off the Social and he's popping up Ponty Pantin later to show them off. Of course he'll 'ave a few snorters up the club, he'll be minging by the time he gets home tonight.

Elsie 'ave had a win on the horses. She's won £500 and she's given me a fiver to spend on myself. She's such a good friend.

Tuesday

I'm awaiting a 'phone call from Shantelll and Philll, I hope they are doing OK out there in 'olland and I can't wait to see the film when it comes out. I wonder, will it be shown in the Odeon in Ponty Pantin? Shantelll doubts it. She reckons it'll be out on video only. Well there's posh for ew, innit? I'll 'ave to rent it from the shop up the high street.

Dai is so proud of his new trousers from the Social. When he takes them off, he keeps them in the china cabinet.

Philll is adamant that he wants a boat. He saw that Derek Brockerly on the telly doing the weather on a boat the other week and Philll would like a big yacht and lots of seamen to help him do the sails. I hope he gets what he wants. He usually does.

Netty is still here, she's doing my head in.

Wednesday

Idwal 'ave had a right gutsful and he's sending Netty away for a week to a health farm so he can 'ave a rest. She wants more children. You know the story, she's round the twist. 76 years old and she believes that she's had a baby and she's nursing the ferret at the moment. Well, that's enough to send anyone demented. Idwal said he can't wait to get himself up the club and he's taking a sleeping bag with him, just in case.

Shantelll phoned and I asked her if she enjoyed the lava bread, but she told me that Philll was spreading it over some Dutch chap's body. Well it's full of iron, it'll do the chap a power of good. I told our Philll not to waste it, it's awful dear, but he's a good boy, he hasn't wasted any of it at all. He's eaten the lot.

I 'aven't seen a clip of Idwal since that Netty has gone to the health farm. I reckon he'll be back soon enough when the club shuts. Next thing Idwal turns up at the mansion with a right tartie woman. Make up an inch thick and a brain the same. Anyway, they disappeared up the stairs and he said, "I'm off to park my bike in the bike shed. Good night."

Thursday

It's awful quiet here: no Philll, no Shantelll, no surgery, no moaning and groaning. I'll be glad when the rag and bone man comes around. I've got a lovely bit of copper piping for him that Dai nicked from the council. If it's not nailed down, it's our Dai's.

I'm doing Dai's favrite today: boil in the bag beef slices in gravy, in a bread roll. He loves it. Mind you, our Philll is a big meat eater, I've never seen him eat but our Shantelll tells me everything. God, I miss them and since she's gone to foreign parts my shopping bill has trebled. I'll never understand how she gets so much food in for such little money. Boy, she's got an eye for a bargain.

I've changed all the bedding here in the house, just in case the doctor calls. Well you never know, do you? Mind you our Philll is very particular, he's had a bidet fitted in the surgery and he's never off it. Cleanliness is next to godliness that's what I do say.

Friday

The big day has arrived: Philll and Shantelll are arriving home. Dai can't wait for his cart load of fags and 'bacco. He can't smoke a British fag now, he says they taste different. Philll 'phoned me from 'olland on his mobile and I asked him, "'ave you got plenty of fags?" He said to me, "Yes Mam, but I can't talk now. I'm in the airport toilets." Oh, I can't wait for him to come home.

The table is laid and our Shantelll 'ave laid a few in her time, mind she could 'ave been a silver service waitress let me tell you. Well, later on that evening in they burst, laden with goodies. Oh, I love a stack of fags in the house, you can get a lot done when you've got fags in. Mind, I do give a packet to the window cleaner and he does the windows extra special like.

I asked our Shantelll when could we see the film they had made and she reckons that it's only on sale in Soho in London. Well that's marvellous, my daughter and son, London film stars. I reckon we should run a trip up to London from the village for everyone to see them. Then I could brag that my children 'ave done well. And Dai is such a good father, he'll do anything I tells him. Shantelll always says men are like floor tiles: lay them right in the beginning and you can walk over them for the rest of your life.

Idwal

All Change
* WEEK 7 *

WELL HELLO MY LOVELIES, how are you this week? Well what a week it was last week, what with our Philll and our Shantelll filming in Amsterdam. What next I ask myself – *Pobol y Cwm?* I can just see our Shantelll on *Songs of Praise.* Anyway, here goes...

Saturday

We're all fed up of smoking fags from 'olland. Give me a good roll, that's what I do say and I can't wait to see the video of the film our Philll and Shantelll made. I wonder if it will be on SC4 the Welsh. You never know.

Philll is so busy since he's back it's like he's had a second burst. He's bought a lot of new things for his business from 'olland and a new air pump to blow up things. Must be for his tyres.

Anyway, Shantelll's husband Paco is after a new job here in the Mumbles and it's a good job by the sound of it: teaching Spanish in a night class. Shantelll said, "If he's working in the nights, so am I." She's always liked working night shift. I always remember when she had a flat up the estate, there was always someone popping back and fore to see her, she's such a popular girl. It was always an open house with our Shantelll.

Anyway, I can't wait to go on our next 'oliday. Philll is paying for me and Dai to go. He's doing so well, but there's no way that we are going away without the help of the Social, so I'm off on Monday to visit the hardship section. Look out.

Sunday

Well it's like Piccadilly Circus here today. The men that are back and fore to our Philll's is unbelievable. Thank God that Simon is back working for him, he must be picking up a good wage and paying his tax like a good boy. I heard our Philll talking to him about a p69 or something like that. Must be a hard one to fill in but never fear, our Dai is good with forms, he knows everything there is to claim for from the Social. He could be an advisor if he wanted.

Elsie's Rex is a good boy. He'll do anything for Elsie. He thinks the world of her, and she's taking him up the club this afternoon, up in Ponty Pantin. There's bingo on and a stripper, nobody can entertain like our Elsie, she knows the good life alright. I means to say, who wants to sit on a beach all day in the sun and eat melon? I reckon it's the best thing that boy has done coming over here. Of course he's not going into the army now since he's here with us, as you know the boys 'ave to do two years in Spain in the army. Philll seemed interested in that. Anyway, Elsie and Rex are getting married, so he can stay here and miss out on the forces. We're not daft.

Had a lovely dinner today: a tin of mince over chips. Lush.

Monday

I'm off down the Social today and I've got my old ripped dress on and a hyper plastic bag, with my old set of broken teeth in. I'm also wearing my broken glasses, the ones with a piece of plaster holding them together. So off I goes in Malcolm's taxi, he drops me off about a mile from the Social office and I get a bus to the door, not to show too much like, innit? In I goes, coughing and limping and this lovely man saw me and we talked through the glass. I said to him, "It's a good job there's a sheet of glass between us, I wouldn't like you to catch anything off me. Cough cough. Our house in Ponty Pantin is so damp and the wallpaper is falling off the walls, the sheets are falling apart."

The man asked where do I keep my towels. I said to him, "Well, the ones that are not thread bare we keep in the green house, because it's the warmest place we 'ave." Then he asked me, where does my husband sleep. I said to him, "In a neighbour's house because it's warmer in there than in ours," and then he asked, "Where do you keep your sheets?" So I told him, "In the sheet house next to the airing cupboard."

Anyway, I did well, we've had a decorating grant, two clothes grants, money to buy glasses and money for towels and extra money for heating because Idwal is an old gripper. I never mentioned the mansion in the Mumbles, best they know nothing about that, innit?

Tuesday

I'm chuffed. We've wangled all that money out of the Social and I'm off to book our 'oliday. I quite fancy the Caribbean, they say it's nice out there. Look out, here we come. Philll has paid for me and Dai and the money from the Social will pay for Maxine Roxanne and Cadwalider. I must remember to tap that Netty for a couple of grand, I'll 'ave to get our Shantelll on the case, she'll spin her a good one, probably about a life saving operation or something like that. I'll be glad to get away soon because the fags are coming to an end and Dai's only got rolling 'bacco left.

Shantelll has landed herself £1,500 pounds from that Netty. She told her she needed to put Cadwalider in a private school so he could learn Spanish to speak to his stepfather Paco. She knows all the tricks. Then she painted a tattoo on her arm and Netty gave her the money to 'ave it removed, wow that girl never ceases to amaze me.

I must remember to buy those funny plugs so I can plug my hair dryer in when we're out in foreign parts. Pity for them really, they can only afford two prongs for their electric out there, not like us here with three.

Wednesday

We've never been out to the Caribbean before, so I'm not going to be a fool on this 'oliday. I'm taking plenty of woollies with us, you never know do you? I'm not getting caught and I'm going to take a lot of Hot Lemons with me. I can't wait for the big day to arrive. I'm so lucky to 'ave such a good family.

We had a stunning tea today: rissoles with curry sauce over the top of them and a stack of bread and butter as well. Only the best for my lot. God I do go through some sliced loaves in this house. I hope they've got plenty of sliced loaves out there in the Caribbean.

Cadwalider is nearly 15 months old and he's had his second tattoo and he's got a fabluss pair of leather trousers. Shantelll is such a good mother. I can see him turning out like our Philll. Duw, our Philll works non stop, 24 hours a day, open all hours. That's my boy, not frightened of a bit of hard work, which reminds me I owe him a packet of wet wipes that I borrowed off him the other day to remove my makeup. He's so handy to 'ave around, nothing's too much for him.

Thursday

We've had a copy of the video that Philll and Shantelll 'ave made over in 'olland. There's one scene that's really good with our Shantelll in it, with this fella in a suit in an office and she's the secretary. Mind you, I 'aven't seen his face yet but he seems a nice boy, lovely brief case. I must get a new pair of glasses soon. Philll had to do a wrestling scene with this big body builder, our Philll never stood a chance against him. He was pinned down in this field for ages. Never mind, maybe in his next film he'll 'ave the leading part.

I'm running a few copies off to send to our Slab, Dai's sister. She'll be ever so proud and I'll 'ave to send one off to America to Netty's brother Waylon in Texas, he likes a good love story.

Mind, I'm a little worried about Philll's friend Rapheal, he seems left out a little bit. He never gets to see our Philll at all. I told him straight, "Go down the surgery and give him some support. He's glad of a hand out, with what he's got to do." I told our Philll, "Rapheal is feeling a bit left out, can't you find him an opening with you down there? He'll fit in tidy I'm sure." Philll didn't seem too forth coming about that idea, I suppose it's best to leave well alone, I'd hate anyone to come between the both of them.

Friday

Shantelll has gone nuts with that money from Netty. She's bought all sorts: tights, lingerie, brassieres, balloons, stilettos and a cigarette holder. Damn she looks the business type with that in her gob. I told our Philll to get one. It would suit him, it's just the thing for a fag.

Rapheal is in a foul mood. He's told Dai that he's sick of faggots. Funny that, we 'aven't had faggots for a good while now. He must be munching elsewhere.

Dai looks lush in his new charity shop trousers, mind you our Elsie had to put a piece in the back again for him, he's put on so much weight. It's all the good living we 'ave, I'm telling you.

Yes life is good for us Jenkins's's's's's. The only thing is that I'm a little worried about our Idwal, he's got piles terrible and the doctor 'ave given him some cream to rub in. It said on the tube, 'Rub on back passage twice daily'. Well we 'aven't got a back passage, so he rubbed a bit behind the front door and for all the good it's done he might as well shove it somewhere else.

All Change
* Week 8 *

Hiya loves, it's Gladys here with the doings that 'ave 'appened here in Ponty Pantin.

Don't talk to me about Spain, wait till I tell you, and we've decided to 'ave some new furniture. We're having two new Chesterfields. Mind you, Dai used to smoke them years ago. Anyway, here goes...

Saturday

Our Dai 'ave sat in that armchair now for the last 18 years and it's gone through. The 3 piece was the only thing we brought to the mansion 'cause he wouldn't part with it. Well, now there's a hole in it and we 'ave to 'ave a new suite, so I gets straight on to Willy – he's into allsorts. Our Philll wants a couple of Chesterfields, well if they're good enough for Fred Elliot they're good enough for us, I say, they're good enough for us...

Anyway, Willy said not to fret, he'd sort it out and not to worry about the money. Oooh, I was landed. Our Philll has such good taste. Chesterfields will look nice in here.

Shantelll is off to town today to get some more baby clothes in Mothercare. She'd better not go nicking again. She was lucky the last time, she nicked the right size.

Rapheal is a lovely boy and is getting on well with our Philll. They must love country and western, well what else is that whip under their bed for? God job they 'aven't got a horse under there as well!

We had a 'phone call from Willy in Swansea to tell us that the Chesterfields are arriving tonight, so I 'ave to get the place ready to fit them in like. God, there's a cuffuffle. We slung the old furniture out the front, which left us with nothing to sit on, but I'm sure it will be worth it.

Later on that evening our Willy pulls up in a van with his three mates, I think they came from tattooland, pretty markings mind, and in came the Chesterfields. Damn they look classy. I could 'ave Catherine Zeta Jones here now.

Sunday

Got up and started the dinner, nothing changes does it? But oh, them Chesterfields looked fab, so I thinks to myself, I must show these off to the neighbours. So I invites Elsie and Rex, Caprice next door and that new woman with the funny shaved hair, they call her Les, it must be short for Leslie. Anyway, out comes the pasting table, I covers it with a big cloth and gets the candelabra out from the china cabinet. Proper posh see!

Shantelll had lamb chops on the knock from an old school friend that worked down the Co-op. Later on that day we all sat and ate the dinner and I kept saying to Caprice, "Would you like to sit on our new red Chesterfields?" So she did and so did Elsie and Rex. Oh, I was made up posing.

I turns on the telly, I can't miss the BBC news, so we all sits there listening to Jamie Owen, then all of a sudden it came on that a factory outlet in Swansea was robbed of two Chesterfields and you'll never guess what: the news also said that a load of tyres 'ave been pinched as well. Well, they weren't under my stairs and the nice Mr Owen said if you are offered cheap tyres to contact the police straight away. I means, could you imagine if someone said to me, 'Would you like four tyres for 15 quid?' Well I mean to say, in your dreams baby, get them in here!

All in all it was a lovely day. Mind you, I wanted to invite that Jamie Owen up for a bit of dinner one day, I'd better not now though!!!

Monday

There was a bang on the door, so off I goes thinking, I hope this isn't the Social or the police, and there they were stood as brazen as anything: Maria and Manwel from Spain. They love coming here, they love the carpets. So I calls them in and they wanted to know where Rex was, so I said, "He's up with Elsie," – in more ways than one I thought to myself. Maria asked, "What's he up to in there?" So him being a carpenter, I tells her that he's been erecting a few things for her. Maria then said, "Is he getting paid?" So I said, "Yes of course." Maria said, "Well I wouldn't like to see him get in a hole with no money coming in." Anyway, they scooted off to a hotel in town and I'm left here wondering what's gonna 'appen next.

Philll won't leave the Chesterfields alone, he loves the smell of leather, always 'ave since he was a little boy. Funny mind, there's no sign of those two next door. Rex must be out doing a bit of tongue and groove innit?

Had an early night. Put all the lights out, just in case that Spanish couple turned up again.

Tuesday

Our Shantelll went out shopping in the old banger and when she was trying to park it she hit another parked car and damaged it a lot. Anyway, she left a note on the other car which said: 'Reversed into your car as I was trying to park, there were lots of witnesses so I thought I'd better leave a note. I bet they all thought I was leaving my name and address so you could get in touch with me.'

Mind you, I'd never cross our Shantelll, especially when she's got the pmt's. In fact, what's the difference between Shantelll with pmt and a rottweiler? Lipstick!

Anyway, Rex turns up with his beloved Elsie, so I tells them that his parents are here. Rex looked a little troubled and with that Maria and Manwel turns up at the door and had stern words with him.

Well, to cut a long story short, he told them that he was staying with Elsie as an odd job man because it's full in our house. Maria was pleased and agreed that it's better to 'ave Rex at hand than having to 'ave a man in from goodness knows where. She seemed quite happy and Rex is still in the will. Mind you, who would want a house in Spain? Think of the cost of putting in all those carpets.

Wednesday

Maria and Manwel went to the airport to go back to Spain feeling quite contented that Rex was in good hands and earning a few bob.

Mind you, I must tell you, Dai said to me at breakfast this morning, "I hope you appreciate that I was quiet coming in last night from the club." So I told him, "Yes you were, but the two that were carrying you weren't, they made an 'ell of a racket."

As you know, I've got a little part-time cleaning job up the club and I noticed the other day that they've got a new sign up behind the bar. It says: 'Drink Canada Dry'. Duw, our Shantelll would love it there, but all jokes aside, Shantelll is working very hard at the moment with our Philll.

I remember when Philll and Shantelll were small I used to bath them together and they used to enjoy splashing away in the bath tub. I remember Philll saying to her, "Mine's better than yours." Shantelll said back to Philll, "Huh, Mammy said with one of these I can 'ave as many of them as I like." She's a girl mind.

Thursday

Pay day today, wages and the Giro, so I'm off to town to buy Elsie an adjustable spanner for her gas meter, she's worn the other one out.

Mind you, I'm awful worried about our Idwal, he's got kidney stones. The doctor reckons there's enough to build an extension, love him. Poor Philll has cut his hand terrible so he went to the doctor and showed him the cut. The doctor told him that he had a foreign body there, well our Philll couldn't get over it, doctors today are so clever aren't they?

Rex 'ave got terrible flu and the doctor told Elsie that it's very contagious and to make sure she doesn't catch it. "Always wash your hands and wear a mask," he said. So later on I went up to Elsie's to see if I could do anything to help and I asked her how his appetite was. She told me, "Well he has toast for breakfast, cheese on toast for dinner, Marmite on toast for tea and jam on toast for supper." I said to her, "He eats a lot of toast doesn't he?" Elsie said, "That's all I can get under the door."

Friday

Bingo night tonight up the club. I'm no good mind, I couldn't win an argument, but our Shantelll is really lucky. She went in to see the bingo caller in the committee room the other day and she had £100 in her hand when she came out. Duw, it's nice to pick a bit up now and then innit? Mind you, our Idwal is going down the Social today to see if he can get some more money out of them. He's pleading insanitry.

Well, when I went out the front door, our old suite had gone. I thought to myself, that's quick for the council mind, but our Shantelll told me all. She saw that smelly family from down the road carrying it into their house. Typical!

Philll 'ave got an underwear party tonight in the front room and he've arranged for models to pose in the garments. He's as good as gold, he's put away a pair of leather briefs for Dai with a zip on the front. He'll love them, he can keep them for best, to go to court or chapel.

The new Holiday Season

* WEEK 1 *

WELL HELLO MY LOVELIES. What fun we've had this week in the boat what Philll 'ave bought. Philll called it 'The Gay Sailor' because we are so happy, all of us. Swansea marina has warned Idwal about flushing the toilet in the marina, he did the same when we were on the train when it was standing in the railway station. You'd think a heard of camels had been there. Anyway, here goes…

Saturday

We are all on our way to the marina in Swansea to go on Philll's new boat and we've got a fabluss picnic hamper, Shantelll ordered it from the catalogue and the fella that delivered it to her told her to 'phone up the catalogue people and tell them that she hadn't received it. Shantelll must be doing a bit of sewing for him.

Anyway, we gets to the marina and on the boat we goes, oh damn it's got a lovely little kitchen and two lush bedrooms. Just then Dai shouted at Shantelll with a broom stick under his arm, "Miss Purity would ye like a parrot or a cockatoo?" Idwal butted in tell her to 'ave a parrot for a change. I don't understand that at all, why would she prefer a parrot? A cockatoo is much more fun, they talk more. Strange old man. Anyway, I'm preparing egg and chips on board. Damn, you can't beat the good life can you? We've got thick bread and marge.

We're off to Flat Holm. Mind you, the coast people told us that we couldn't get off the boat, we had to 'ave permission to go on the island. They should let us off the boat, they could do with a bit of class. Dai wants to sail to France to get some fags. I can see another business opening up before long: 'Philll's Fags – Imported and Cheap'. Good luck to him I say.

Shantelll has invited the man from up the petrol station on board, we've got to keep in with him, what with the price on petrol and all that. She'll sort him out.

We dropped anchor just outside Swansea Bay and we all went to bed for the night.

Sunday

I woke about five and twenty to nine in the morning and I went up on deck to see what the weather was doing. All of a sudden I couldn't see the Mumbles. The anchor rope had snapped and we had drifted out to sea. Mind you, I was landed. We was by Barry Island. We could 'ave ended up in the south of France, but no, Barry Island it was. I said, "Quick Dai, get the dingy out and let's go to bingo."

Anyway, we gets to shore on this dingy and we goes for a cheap breakfast. Lush! Then off we went to bingo for the day. We made our way back to the boat, loaded with teddy bears. What a wonderful day. Thank goodness Philll had bought a spare anchor with him. We gets on board and off we went back to Swansea. Shantelll tied two teddy bears to a buoy. Aw, they looked as if they'd eloped.

The waves were splashing a little bit, so I said to Philll, "Mind you don't get the boat wet, mind." He said, "Mam, don't go on. I 'aven't started work yet, give me a chance will you?" We got back in time to catch the last session of bingo in Swansea. Shantelll called a £250 house and she took us all for a meal out.

Monday

Well what a day it was yesterday. Boat, bingo, boat, bingo – fabs.

I've decided to take in a few lodgers, it'll help pay for the mooring costs for the boat, so I've advertised in the paper: 'Lodgers look no further', we'll see who turns up.

Well no sooner than the paper was out there and there was

a 'phone call from a young gentleman. He wanted to rent one of the rooms. I told him to call down and see us. About an hour later there was a knock on the door, so I answered it and there was this lovely young chap. God he looked exactly like Brad Pitt. He said to me, "What a lovely house you 'ave. I'm glad there's no steps, I've got a terrible bad back." I jumped on the case straight away. I told him, "Fear not, my son is a doctor and he has his own surgery here. I'm sure he'll squeeze you in if he can." Well the chap was landed and off he went into Philll's surgery. About an hour later he came out, all smiles. "I'll take the room Mrs," he said. I said to him, "But you 'aven't seen it yet." That boy could recognise class a mile off let me tell you.

Tuesday

Shantelll 'ave got to see to two rugby players this morning. They need a good rub down. Anyway, they turns up, well I've never seen two bigger blokes in my life. They must 'ave been about 6ft 5 the both of them and they must 'ave weighed 16-17 stone. In they went and there was our Shantelll in her nurses uniform, damn she looked smart, well about an hour and a half later they came out, the two of them puffing and panting. They could hardly stand and they said to me, "God, Mrs, we could do with a 'oliday after that." "There you are then," I said to them. "You can't beat the best. Our Shantelll is very well qualified you know." Anyway, off they went totally knackerated and out came our Shantelll and said to me, "Mam, make us a cup of tea, I've got two more to see in half an hour." She's like a horse our Shantelll.

The new Holiday Season
* WEEK 2 *

WELL HELLO MY LOVELIES, it's Gladys here with the 'appenings that 'ave 'appened in the life of the Jenkins's's's's's

Dai 'ave bought a fishing rod, look out the waters of Wales, and Shantelll has got to visit some people. I'll tell you more about that later. Here goes...

Saturday

I've had a gutsful of that boat. The weather is so unpredictable here isn't it? You should 'ave seen Philll the other day on the boat. Up and down, up and down. I hope his big end will stand up to it all. The next thing we'll find is a couple of oars on there. You can never tell what's next with our Philll.

I've got tumps of washing to do. I 'ave to wash Dai's underpants – all three pairs of them – well you can't be to particular can you? Our Dai says he'd like to change them once every week whether he needed to or not.

Shantelll is pressing her clothes for some meeting that's coming up this week, one with the bank manager, one with the mechanic and one with a fisherman. We'll see what she pulls off. Nothing's too much for our Shantelll.

Idwal 'ave bought new long johns for the trip to the Caribbean and Netty's bought an electric blanket. The ferret is doing well at nursery school. His Welsh is coming half tidy. The school pacifies Netty and the ferret because she pays them good money. Well you can't blame them can you?

Sunday

Shantelll is still pressing her clothes. These meetings must be really important. I wonder what she's up to? Whatever it is, I pity any fella that crosses her. Shantelll always sorts people out if they start getting stroppy. She always gets her own way, but she's always polite. She ends her conversations, even after an argument, by saying, "Oh by the way, how's your wife these days then?" They always back off and she's got a lovely big photo album of all her clients, just in case they want a souvenir.

She's got a few clients coming to see her today and she's reading their future. She's reading the tea leaves, she's such a talented girl. She gets it all from her mother see. Of course I'm a Merthyr girl at heart. Anyway these two fellas turns up and they asked if Madam Shanters was here. I guessed that was her stage name, so I takes them into the front room where it was all dark and dingy. There was our Shantelll, oops I means Madam Shanters, looking into a crystal ball she's nicked off some piece in a caravan in town last week. Anyway, in they settled and I got on with the dinner.

She told the two blokies that they would meet a new person in their lives and this woman would be coming. Soon. The one man said to her, "You're very cocksure of yourself." Shantelll said, "I always am love." Anyway, they legged it and they seemed quite happy. Our darling Madam Shanters got £75 off them both. Such an enterprising girl she is. She told our Philll that he would meet a tall dark handsome stranger. Philll just yawned and said, "I'd better get back to work then hadn't I?"

Monday

Shantelll is off to the three meetings today and I'm here helping Philll out as a receptionist. I must admit there's a varied cross of clientele that comes here, all sorts. I bet his hands take a hammering with all those bad backs. His hands are rough as anything: full of chaps. I must buy some of that Magno soap for him.

The next thing our Shantelll bursts into the room, happy as Larry. She's seen the bank manager and she's got the overdraft limit that she wanted. "Oh Mam," she said. "Don't talk to me about money, see the wad on him, lush. And the fisherman has given me a weekly supply of fish, he had lovely tackle, and the mechanic is going to personally look after my new sports car. He had a lovely set of tools he did Mam." Our Shantelll will get on in life I'm telling you now. She wants to expand out on her own in business. Now she's got the car she could open up anywhere.

Tuesday

Philll 'ave asked me to get some oil for his handcuffs. He still likes to play cops and robbers. He's a little boy at heart you know.

Philll 'ave got a fella coming in to see him from Switzerland, so I thought seeing that I was on reception duty I would cut up a Swiss roll, just to make him feel at home.

Our Philll do go through some tissues, he uses boxes of them. He's gone through nine boxes this morning. He must be coming down with a cold love him. He should 'ave Vic on his chest.

I've made a lovely tea for us tonight: bread and gravy with peas. Lush.

Wednesday

Dai 'ave had a gutsful of Swansea. He wants to go back to the valleys. He misses the club and I must admit, so do I. I miss getting my slimming tablets from there and of course the gossip. Dai 'ave got an hole in his trousers, so I'm taking them back to the charity shop. I mean to say, I paid £1.50 for them. No way hose. They're going back by hook or by crook.

The betting shop 'ave put a limit on our Idwal, he wins so much. So he's dressing up in a false moustache and a beard to put his bets on.

Shantelll 'ave gone for the day to the zoo with Netty and they went to visit the sharks. Netty looked in through the glass and looked at the big sharks and she said to Shantelll, "Would they eat me whole?" And Shantelll said back to her, "No Net. They spits that out." Mind you there was a fella there with a harpoon, massive it was. Shantelll couldn't get over the size of his weapon, but there you are, you need it just in case, don't you?

They had a lovely day at the zoo until it was time to come home and that Netty started creating. She wanted a monkey for company for Jason the ferret. There was ructions there, thank God that our Shantelll got her out of there in time.

Thursday

Netty the sly old bag 'ave nicked a baby monkey from the zoo and it's been Brad Pitting all over the house. It's 'umming here. If she didn't own the mansion I'd throw her out. So I've phoned the zoo to come and get it back. I've locked it in the bread bin for the moment until the zoo keeper gets here. I hope Dai don't come in early and go to make a sandwich.

Anyway, the zoo blokie turns up and takes the baby monkey back. Netty created again, she was shouting, "He's taking my child, he's taking my baby!" Idwal calmed her down with a glass of Pimms and whisked her upstairs.

Netty is going to a parents' meeting tonight about Jason the ferret. The school 'ave said that he's quite good at Welsh but a bit slow with his maths, he must be following Dai.

Friday

I'm still on reception duty and I'm expecting a fella from the States to arrive anytime. Philll said he was from Tucson in Arizona. I told him when he arrived, "This is a long way for you to come isn't it?" He just smiled. "It'll be worth it madam," he said. Fancy him calling me madam, no sense at all.

Shantelll has gone down to the marina in Swansea to see some seamen I expect. She loves the sailor boys she does. Dai 'ave had his new fishing rod and he's been using it to nick underpants from next door's line. Well it'll save me buying new won't it?

The new Holiday Season

* WEEK 3 *

WELL HELLO MY LOVELIES, it's Gladys here with the 'appenings that 'ave 'appened here in the Mumbles. Shantelll has got her pen friend coming over from 'olland, the woman she met when she was filming out there. Claudia she's called. Anyway, here goes…

Saturday

Shantelll is all busy getting the guest suite ready for her Dutch friend. Our gardener is busy as well cutting the acres of lawns that we 'ave. Philll is sipping Champain on the terrace, Idwal is having his feet done by the chiropodist and Dai's gone to post a letter off to the Social for an increase as his bad back is getting badder.

Our Shantelll has had the family allowance and has had another tattoo done on Cadwalider, damn he looks lush. Netty, well she's still putting years on Idwal and the rest of us with her moans and groans. Our Dai's butty Nobby is coming around later on with some fags on the knock: £25 a carton. Tidy, and he's got some booze as well for our parties now that the weather is decent.

I told our Shantelll to show this Dutch girl the mountains as they 'aven't got any themselves, God love them, and maybe we'll take her out on the boat. Duw, life is tough when you're on the Social. Mind you our Philll is doing well, what with his surgery in Ponty Pantin and the one in the bay in sin city and he's opened one here in the stables in Mumbles. And of course the mobile bad back unit Squeals on Wheels. The money is pouring in. We are actually thinking of moving from here as

Netty has signed the mansion over to Idwal and we fancy living in a 12th century castle, that would suit us. I'm still waiting for Nobby to turn up with the fags, not a sign as yet.

Sunday

I was getting ready for chapel when the front door went, so I checks the magic camera and there he was, Nobby with the fags. Oh, just as well – I'm down to rolls at the minute. I opens the door and says, "Oh my handsome boy, come to Gladys, let's see what you've got." Mind you, he had loads of foreign fags. Our Shantelll picks up a packet with an animal on them and she said, "I've tried everything but nothing satisfies me like a Camel." Our Philll looked at her with disgust and pealed his poloney with great accuracy. We took the lot off Nobby, well our Philll always says you can't beat a good fag after doing the doings.

Dai had to go and visit the doctor today, private like, that's why he can go on a Sunday. Money talks mind and the doctor said to him, "Your blood pressure is sky high and your cholesterol is through the roof. I'd better get you something to calm you down." Dai told him straight, "Pass me an ashtray doc." The doctor played hell with our Dai but Dai was adamant, he was going over the bookies with his fags and to 'ave a skinful later. You can't keep a good man down, mind you. That's what our Philll always says after work.

Monday

This Dutch piece has arrived and boy is she tall, about 7ft 9. And love her, she brought us a load of fags as she don't smoke. Dai was landed. "Don't you smoke?" Dai said. "Nay," she said. Then Dai said, "Gladys you'd better pitch a tent for her otherwise she'll choke in here."

Then Philll intervened and said, "Mam, don't worry, Claudia can stay in the surgery and help me out, there's plenty of beds and she can do her eye makeup lying down as the mirrors are on the ceiling." I thought to myself, what a good idea, our Philll is always coming up with good ideas.

So in she goes and unpacks her case.

Idwal asked Claudia if she was in a children's book years ago, if she was the one that stuck her finger in a dyke. "No," I says to our Idwal, "that was a little boy called Peter. Peter and the dyke." Philll looked bewildered at the thought. "What a waste," he said. Mind you, I do agree with him, she could 'ave done better for herself, maybe as an 'oliday rep.

Anyway, there's no sign of Claudia, so I says to our Philll, "Where's that poor little Dutch girl?" He said, "Mam, she's not so poor now."

Tuesday

Claudia is still in the surgery, we 'aven't seen a clip of her. I asked our Philll if she would like something to eat. Philll reckons she's already had her fill.

Shantelll took Dai out in the soft top sports car and as they were driving along a seagull pooed on Dai's head. Shantelll stopped the car and said to Dai, "Hang on Dad, I'll get some toilet roll out." Dai said, "Don't be daft girl, the seagull will be miles away by now." But Dai was thrilled really, he said that the poo poo was an omen and he stopped off to buy an extra lottery ticket.

No sign of Claudia, perhaps she's shy, mind you these Dutch people are very shy and quiet aren't they? They don't see much at all except tulip fields. They can't see much life, God love them. Mind you, Shantelll told me that her family owns an opium den. She should feel quite at home by here with all these smoking.

Wednesday

Claudia popped her head out of the surgery and called up to the kitchen for a cuppa. I thought to myself, I bet she feels homesick, I'll try and cheer her up. So I says to her, "'olland is a lovely place. It's a county of Germany, isn't it?" She looked at me a bit fierce like, so I rammed a Welsh cake in her gob and told her to chill.

She told me that she came from Rotterdam, so I said very

kindly back to her, "Well I hope all your dams don't rot love, it must be the damp." She seems a nice enough girl but the fags she smokes smell awful and she rolls them herself. I can't understand it: one minute she smokes and the next she doesn't. I wish she'd make up her mind. Then she said to me, "Hey Gladys baby, I'm off down to help Philll with some more clients, cool man." Fancy calling me a man! Pie and chips will cure her, you wait and see.

Thursday

The school 'ave phoned for Netty to come and collect the ferret from the playground as he 'ave bitten two children and the school's policy is no biting. Most definitely I'll 'ave to tell Netty to 'ave a private tutor for the ferret, or Jason as she calls him. That'll sort the problem out.

Shantelll 'ave offered to teach maths and Welsh to the ferret for a nominal fee paid a term in advance. Netty jumped at the idea and paid our Shantelll in cash straight away. That girl can make a living out of nothing. Philll always says she should open up in Merthyr, mind you I love Merthyr. I'm a Merthyr girl, I'm from the Gurnos. Oh I do miss it terrible, there's a better class of people up there than anywhere else. I'd love to move back there. I used to work in Hoovers years ago and drink in the ex-serviceman's club on the rounderbout. Oh they could pull a fantastic pint of Dark up there. Yes, it's Merthyr for me. Every time!

Friday

Well to be honest I 'aven't seen a lot of this Claudia girl. I was going to take her out on the boat and for a drive with Shantelll up Merthyr way to show her the sights, but she seems preoccupied with something or other down that surgery. Maybe she wants to train as a nurse, you never know.

Shantelll took her out into Swansea city centre to do a bit of shopping for when she goes back to 'olland. Every shop that Shantelll went into they came out loaded and our Shantelll gave her a diamond necklace worth about four grand. Our Shantelll is dull to the core, she'd rather give than take.

Shantelll looks pleased with herself. Claudia has given her a letter to go back out to 'olland and make another film, It's called *GBH – Grunting Behind Hedges*. I hope our Shantelll can hack it, she's never been very good with trees and plants.

Philll

The new Holiday Season

* WEEK 4 *

WELL HELLO MY LOVELIES, it's Gladys here with the 'appenings that 'ave 'appened here in this wonderful mansion in the Mumbles, and you'll never guess what Shantelll has gone and bought – a motor home. Well I'll tell you about it later, it's fantastic. Dai wants to use it to sell burgers when there's a match on. Oh God, here goes...

Saturday

Shantelll 'ave decided to buy a motor home. It's a caravan in a van and she's adamant that she's having one. I said to her, "Shantelll why are you buying one of these motor homes? Aren't you happy here in the Mumbles?" She said back to me, "Of course I am Mam, but I fancy traipsing around and 'ave a 'oliday wherever I want. Merthyr is nice this time of year," she said. She also said something about going to Upper Cwmtwrch for a weekend break. Well, when our Shantelll has got an idea in her head that's it, nothing will move her. So she took our Dai with her to Cardiff to 'ave a look at these motor homes. Dai told her to get one with a serving hatch on the side so they could serve burgers when there's a match on somewhere. She wasn't fussed on that, anyway, she's bought one. It cost her £30,000, she must 'ave done well with her tips in the surgery. Anyway, home she comes in this new motor home. I must admit it's lush mind.

Sunday

No sign of our Shantelll. She was out the front in the motor home sleeping and apparently a fella broke in in the middle of the night and he didn't get out for two and a half hours. Mind you, it is a big one. You can get lost in it. I must admit, our Shantelll is not frightened of anything nor anyone. She's out for herself, but she has got a heart of gold. She'll pinch anything for anyone, love her.

Shantelll has had painted on the side: 'Mystical Madam Shanters' and she's off around the whole of Wales. Look out Neath Fair, that's all I can say. Mind you, we are all tempted to go abroad in it – that would be nice and we could take lava bread over to the continent and educate those French and Dutch: Duw, they'd love it.

There's a chemical toilet in the motor home and it's portable – you can put it in the bathroom or in the bedroom. It's marvellous and when she's finished using it she puts a little cloth over it and then puts a bowl of fruit on the top. She's so clever.

Monday

I'm off to town to do a bit of shopping: tripe and onions tonight for supper, Dai loves it and of course I mustn't forget Idwal's chickling. I bought him about two yards of it, beautiful.

I met our Shantelll in town, she's going to pick up a shopping check, you know the ones: 'ave now, pay a bit later. So she goes into this big department store and tells this piece all her details. The woman said, "Name?" Shantelll said Susan and her surname was Decaprio. I thought this must be her new stage name. It had a nice ring to it and Shantelll picked up a nice ring: 22 carrot. A bargain she said and off she went back in to the main street, taking off her sunglasses and beauty spot and her head scarf.

A bit later on I called to see our Philll in the surgery in the outhouse behind the mansion. There were quite a few waiting to go in, so I thought I'd do the right thing and offer them a cuppa. They looked a bit dull at me when I asked how their backs were. Probably shy. Never fear, our Philll will get to the bottom of it. His motto is: 'Massage it, rub it and everything will come tidy in the end.'

Tuesday

Dai 'ave been offered a job on the sly, cleaning the eyes out of the potatoes in the chippy. He used to do that before, when they called him 'The Optician' but he ate more chips than he could cut and they sacked him. This time he's really gonna 'ave a go and resist the chips and hold a job down, love him. He can't do much because, as you all know, he's got an incurable bad back. I can see the pain on his face.

The chickling went down a storm. Idwal was chewing it a foot at a time and the tripe is in the oven with some onions we pinched from next door. What we do is, we get our Maxine Roxanne to throw her ball over and she asks can she get her ball back and when she nips in to get it she pulls a couple of onions up from the ground and slings them over ours. Duw, last week she slung some lovely new potatoes over the wall. Shantelll 'ave trained her well. I do tell our Maxine Roxanne to keep her hand on her cherry, but she's adamant there's only onions there.

Wednesday

Elsie and Rex are coming to stay with us. It'll be nice for Rex to see his two Spanish brothers here. Mind you, Elsie 'ave had Rex working like the clappers. He's doing some work on her gas meter. About a week after the gas man has been, he puts a different meter on for about six weeks and then puts the old one back on, just before the gas man calls again. Rex must be practicing to 'ave a job on with the gas board. Mind you it must be working tidy like, she never complains about her bill.

Philll 'ave had a fax machine put in. I said to him, "What's that then?" He explained you can put paper in it and it goes to another fax machine. I thought to myself, that sounds good, so when I was in town later on that day I was thinking of doing a bit of decorating for our Shantelll's room and I wasn't sure which wallpaper to buy. So I goes up to the woman on the counter and asked her, "Can you fax this piece of wallpaper to my house for our Shantelll to see the pattern?" She looked at me twp, but fax it she did and our Shantelll loved it, so

I bought eight rolls. I thought to myself, damn that fax is wonderful. The only trouble is there's a piece of wallpaper by the side of the curtain with a 'phone number on it, but there you are, we nearly got it right!

Thursday

Dai's brother Willy is paying us a visit today, he's been staying up in North Wales, keeping low after a dodgy deal he's done. Mind you, it was fabs to see him. He brought me a load of fags and a case of Dark and two bingo boards from Bangor. I was landed. I cooked him tea and gave him one of the guest rooms, then I downed two cans of Dark and went for a lay down.

I cooked a nice meal for the evening: chicken and stuffing. Philll loves a nice bit of stuffing. He went to a fancy dress party once and was chatting to a fella that was dressed as a turkey. He asked our Philll, "What did you come as?" Philll said to him, "Sage and onions." Ooh, he's an artistic boy alright.

Friday

Tomorrow we are all off to the Caribbean and I 'aven't started packing tidy yet, only the woollies and an anorak each. Idwal is taking an oil-filled radiator with him and Netty's heart broken – she's got to leave the ferret with our Dai's brother Willy. Philll's so exited and he's taking his rubber suit with him. Must want to do some snorkelling I suppose. Shantelll has packed already, she's so organised: two bras, two pairs of knickers, a case of wet wipes and a bottle of hand wash detergent to swill her draws out. Oh yes, and a ton of make up.

Shantelll 'ave had dreadlocks done on our Cadwalider, damn he looks fantastic. He's 18 months now. Dai is taking his portable telly with him as he doesn't want to miss SC4 the Welsh and his snooker and racing results. I hope the aeroplane people don't mind, mind you we are flying with the best, Simple Jet. Marvellous.

Simon is taking over the surgery, he's a great fill-in according to Philll. "Don't let the business go down," I told him. "Work hard and keep your end up because if anything ever 'appened to our Philll's business we'd all end up in a hole."

The new Holiday Season

* WEEK 5 *

Saturday

Well hello my lovelies, how are you? Here we are again on our way for our 'olidays, and today we are off to the Caribbean. We are flying from Jatwick, very posh. Anyway I've done the jam sandwiches ready for the off and 10 flasks of tea as well. We can't wait, mind you we've never been to the Caribbean before, so we've taken all precautions: woollies, thermals, gloves and Idwal's oil-filled radiator.

Anyway, we leave the mansion in Mumbles in the morning and off we go up the M4. Duw, it's a lovely run. We passed sin city, then we gets to the bridge: they didn't stop us for our passports this time but they always stop us on the way back and they charge us just like East Germany.

So we've left good old Wales and here we are in foreign parts: Engaland. Very posh and don't they talk different here? This woman said to me in the services, "'ello me loverrrrr, would ye like a cup of tea me loverrrrr?" Well there's a price on the tea up here, never again

Anyway, we gets to a lovely place called Reding and Swine Don was nice as well. We got to Jatwick Airport, big mind and we parks in the long stay place. Then we makes our way to the departarations segment and our suitcases are taken on board. Mind you, the bloke wanted to know why our Idwal's case was so heavy, but Philll put him right and took him to the toilet to 'ave a chat. Aw love him, he must 'ave been taken short but he came back all smiles and said to us, "Don't worry about the excess. Carry on." Philll exchanged numbers with him and promised to fit him in when he got back. Love him, he must 'ave a bad back, heavy suitcases see.

Our plane has been delayed until tomorrow. Charming! We are whisked off to a posh hotel and we goes to bed after a skinful of free booze.

Sunday

We gets up and makes our way back to the airport and thank God the plane is on time today. Off we goes on board: Philll, Idwal, Shantelll, Cadwalider, Maxine Roxanne, Paco, Rapheal and of course Netty and Dai. What a set we are, but there you are, it's about time that the Caribbean had some classy people like us.

We gets on the plane and Idwal called the flying waitress and asked her for a pint of Dark, but no joy. He had to 'ave a little tin of larger. Philll wanted to know if he could see in to the cockpit. Shantelll told him, "Be'ave Philll, it's not a nightclub." Anyway, this young flussy took our Philll up to the front and in he goes to see the pilots. They were in there ages, next thing the flying waitress was trying to get in the cockpit, but she couldn't, the door was locked from the inside. Philll must have been having cockpit lessons. Anyway about 40 minutes later the door opens and out comes Philll to a round of applause from the cabin crew.

We eventually takes off and Idwal fell asleep, Cadwalider peed on the seat, Maxine Roxanne spewed everywhere and Netty started taking orders for drinks. She was pushing a trolley up and down the aisle. Oh there was uproar, the flying waitresses didn't know if they were coming or going.

When Philll ordered duty free the flying waitress said that there was no charge, the pilot said that it was on him.

Monday

We're still on the plane, they must be going slow or something. I said to the flying waitress, "There's a long time it takes to get to the Caribbean. It only takes us two and a half hours to get to Spain. We're not coming here again unless you get a faster plane next time." I soon put her in her place.

We eventually lands and there's nothing but palm trees and coconuts. I thought to myself, we could 'ave had this in the fun fair. The trees looked lush, mind, just like Madam Yeoman's, beautiful!

We gets to the hotel and Duw, it was boiling hot. Philll sat with his bottom in the fridge. He said he was getting ready for tonight. Shantelll unpacked two pairs of draws, two uplift bras and a packet of Persil and of course two carrier bags of makeup. I've soaked our Cadwalider's clothes and our Maxine Roxanne's clothes in this lovely little washing machine in the bathroom. Very handy I thought. Shantelll looks fabs with her hair in dreadlocks and so does Maxine Roxanne and Cadwalider.

Tuesday

We goes down to the breakfast room in the hotel. It's a very nice hotel called the Hotel Bananas, very exotic, and we orders a breakfast. Dai asked for bacon and lava bread but they just looked daft at him and they brought him some of that cereal stuff, musslee and two coconuts.

Netty is playing up terrible, she's found a monkey and she thinks it's related to her. We're just keeping her happy, anything for a peaceful life.

Shantelll has sent Paco and Rapheal on a Caribbean tour for the day. She's already met up with a lovely young man on a fishing boat and she's off for the day with him. Philll would 'ave gone but he doesn't like fish much.

Idwal is having a Jakkusi, he reckons that he's gonna do the washing in there later on in the week and to boot he's lost his teeth in there as well. We've had half the hotel staff out looking for them. They drained the Jakkusi and eventually they found his teeth at the bottom with two pairs of draws and four pairs of glasses. Dai said, "Well that's where my four pairs of specs went," and grabbed them. Oh he's a boy mind, he'll be selling them up the club when we get back home.

Wednesday

Well to be honest I've had a gutsful already. There's no bingo here, no bookies, no working man clubs. I don't see the attraction. I reckon we should 'ave gone to Porthcawl.

Philll has made friends with a lovely little waiter and we're all having free drinks offa him. Philll is taking him for a guided tour later, mind you Philll's never been here before. Philll must be showing him foreign parts I reckon.

Shantelll is still out fishing. I bet that fisherman will get a good catch out there on the boat. Shantelll said his tackle was fabs, but the only thing I hate is cleaning the fish, and there's not a tidy kitchen in this hotel room. Dai will 'ave to go selling the fish somewhere, that'll fetch him a few bob.

Shantelll came back that evening and said to me, "Oh Mam, what a wonderful time. I had hold of his rod all day."

Thursday

Dai 'ave got the runs and the only thing that cures him is a Woodbine. Thank goodness I've packed a carton in the suitcase. Netty's gone missing with the monkey and the children are selling coconuts on the beach, nice for them. Shantelll is taking her pills, she must 'ave a headache. She said to me, "Mam, I'm glad I've taken my pills, especially after yesterday." She's so sensible.

I'm out buying pressies for the rest of the family. I've bought Elsie a coconut ashtray and Shantelll has bought herself a coconut bra. Idwal said, "That'll keep the milk fresh."

Dai 'ave been on a donkey on the beach but the donkey couldn't move. It sank into the sand, love him and it took six men to get the donkey back out. I've told Dai about his weight but I reckon to be honest that the sand is poor quality here. Anyway, the hotel is doing us a special supper tonight: coconut casserole. Can't wait.

Friday

Got up in the morning and we all had the runs. That's the last time we 'ave coconuts left right and centre. We're leaving today for the airport and to be honest I can't wait to get home to 'ave some tidy faggots.

The plane was on time today, that makes a change and we boards the aircraft loaded with fags, booze and a couple of coconuts for Caprice next door. She's quite often constipated.

We gets back to Jatwick in the evening and we stops for fish and chips, lush. We had mushy peas as well, you can't beat the fine things in life can you? We gets back to the Severn Bridge and them customs stopped us. Dai gave them our passports and they charged us £5.30 duty – only then they lets us through into Wales. And with Dai and Idwal both 'aving disability stickers, we could 'ave got through for bugger all – if either of them had remembered to bring them. I could quite happily throttle the pair of 'em at times.

I must admit, Netty was no trouble at all, she spent the whole of the week with a monkey and it gave our Idwal a bit of a break.

The next time we go away it'll be in Shantelll's motor home. Mind you, Philll wants a motor home now as well. Dai said he'd be better off with a motor homo.

The new Holiday Season

* WEEK 6 *

WELL HELLO MY LOVELIES, how are you this week? Well what a week we had last week in the Caribbean! I much prefer Porthcawl, nicer altogether. Anyway, here goes...

Saturday

We've decided to go on a camping 'oliday this week – we're still in 'oliday mood and they couldn't make a tidy chip out there in the Caribbean. If you remember, we bought a tent ages ago and we've got Shantelll's motor home, so look out England, the Welsh are on the rampage.

I've made sure that we've all got our passports ready to cross over into England and I've told Netty to apply for a visa as she's from the States. We must check to see if the ferret needs inoculations and quarantine to travel. Anyway, we sets off in the motor home and we gets to the bridge (there was no customs there on the way into England so that was a relief) and we makes our way to the West Country. I 'ave to speak slow for them seeing we are foreigners.

We gets to this lovely camp site: 'Camping here' it said. Oh Philll looked really excited and bolted off to the showers as soon as he got there. He's always been very clean mind. Anyway, we didn't see much of Philll so we parks up and there's electric points, water, the lot. A bit like home but with nicer neighbours.

Mind you, if you think we got it easy now, let me tell you over the years I've had it hard. I tried telling our Philll, "You don't know the meaning of hard."

Sunday

No sign of Philll, he must be in the showers still. Shantelll has taken up chess, she's never played it before but the fella that's teaching her is gorgeous and looks a bit like Brad Pitt. I never thought that our Shantelll was into chess but there you are, she must 'ave hidden talents.

Dai has been struggling with the tent to get it looking tidy next to the motor home. He's really good at getting it up but he's having trouble keeping it up, must be the wind.

There's a heated swimming pool here as well and there's a lovely lifeguard called Jason, a big blonde chap with muscles on his spit. Gorgeous he is alright and Philll has paid him for some private tuition to improve his doggy paddle. The thing is with our Philll, when he's in the water he's frightened to open his legs but he's coming slowly, let me tell you.

The stove in the motor home is better than the one in the house, so the stuffed hearts are in and I'm off to the bar while they are cooking. Shantelll came with me for a drink and the people there were right posh. They were drinking these fancy drinks with umbrellas in and cherries and stuff, damn they looked smart. The bar man said to our Shantelll, "Do you like cocktails?" Shantelll said to him, "Yes love, tell me one." Ooh, she's a daft thing let me tell you. You don't talk a cocktail you drink them. Anyway, had one over the odds and staggered back to rescue the stuffed hearts just in time.

Monday

What a fabluss place: there's bingo in the morning, in the afternoon and in the night. Well that's me seen to.

I'm entering a glamorous grandmother competition tonight so look out. I'm busy getting ready and I've got my heated rollers in, ready for the off. Shantelll has met up with two of the judges and had a meeting with them. Boy, they look knackerated already, they'll never make tonight if they look like that now.

I togged up in my new dress from the catalogue,

remembering not to dirty it. I'll send it back when we gets home. I parades up and down this stage and there's a fella playing the organ as well. Oh it's just like the club and the next thing I hear is, "And the winner is Mrs Gladys Jenkins from Wales." Oh I was landed. I had a bowcet of flowers, a box of chocolates and a case of larger. Oh I can't wait, this is going to be a great week.

Tuesday

The local newspaper 'ave come to take my photo, boy oh boy do I feel like a celebrity. I'm sure the photos will look great, I soaked my teeth in bleach for that extra sparkle.

Dai 'ave had a lot of trouble with the tent, I was telling Elsie on the 'phone. I told her, "He's been trying to get it up all night, but in the end I said to him: 'If it goes down love don't worry, I'll get that nice lifeguard over to get it back up'."

Philll 'ave done a terrible mistake and Shantelll is fuming. He's only gone and put petrol in the water supply. Shantelll screamed at him, "That's all you do is put things in the wrong holes." God there was a to do. Anyway, Philll got it sorted with help from that nice judge from the talent show. Philll is seeing him later to buy him a drink. I heard Philll ask him if he fancied a screwdriver.

Wednesday

The larger and the chocolates are going down well. I've cooked a chicken and made a chocolate sauce to go over it. Oh yes, I listen to the Garden programme, nice.

I was wondering: do they 'ave here in England their own Assembly? They ought to 'ave, they seem posh enough. I'm off looking for fags to take home with us but there's not a lot of difference in the price, in fact they are cheaper up the club, half the price actually. Thank God for the lovely club.

I should 'ave brought a phrase book with me. I've picked a few words up mind: 'Ooh aar: where you be from my babarrr?'

Thursday

Dai's runs 'ave slowed up a little bit and believe you me life is difficult enough in a motor home without 'aving Dai and his stomach troubles to boot, but there you are, he's on the mend.

Idwal 'ave met up with a 40-year-old woman from London, she's from Sojo and works nights only. I can't remember what she said her job description was, something about horizontal refreshment or something like that. Do you know our Idwal will worm himself into anywhere. Duw, he's a boy mind.

Mind you our other boys, the Spanish ones, are as good as gold, they're no trouble at all. All they do is wash dishes and make strange coffee and wipe the surfaces all day, handy. Mind you, I can never drink this foreign coffee that they make, I like a good spoonful of the Co-op's best instant. You can't beat it, lush.

The children are enjoying the 'oliday, they're selling fag ends to Dai and he rolls them up again, so they're out all day looking for them. Well it keeps them off the street don't it?

Friday

Home today and I'm gonna play hell with the customs if they charge us to go back into Wales again. We had to pay £5.30 the last time and we weren't over the limit at all. Well I made certain Dai brought his disability sticker with him this time. Funny lot those customs mind.

Shantelll looks as if she's putting on a bit of weight. She reckons she might 'ave picked something up on that fishing boat out in the Caribbean and she looks quite concerned.

Philll 'ave had a good breakfast this morning, he's got to keep his strength up. He's got clients booked tonight in the Mumbles and he can't let anyone down. I told him straight, "Keep your pecker up love and one day you will be able to retire, and then you can lay back and take it easy."

The trouble is he's always on the go, but the money is rolling in. I'm always telling him, "Keep your hands clean and don't get yourself into anything you can't get out of. Be firm and you'll come through in the end." I'm so proud of him.

The new Holiday Season

* WEEK 7 *

WELL HELLO MY LOVELIES, how are you this week? Well what a week we had last week camping and me winning the glamorous granny competition. There's life in this old boot yet, that's what our Dai says to me. Anyway, here goes...

Saturday

Idwal is getting me down a little bit, what with his moaning and groaning, but it's that Netty it is. She wants a bit of nonsense all of the time and poor old Idwal can't keep it up, love him. He can't stand the pace, but she's a good woman. I do believe she's going to give some money to the chapel 'cause I heard her saying the other day to our Idwal that the organ is too small. Idwal told her straight, "It wasn't expected to play in a cathedral." Funny, I didn't know that Idwal was musical.

Shantelll won't get out of that motor home and to be honest it's got a better bathroom than mine indoors. We're having a fabluss tea today: chips and mint sauce, our Shantelll's favrite. She always says that she likes something with a bit of bite to it. I told her straight, "Don't bite off too much now." She don't stop working, but don't tell the Social.

Sunday

Off to chapel today and I've got my new hat on, the one I got off the catalogue. Nice too. Dai said I looks like Cruella de Ville in it. I gets to the chapel and I bows my head down to pray, then I realises that there's two collections and I've only got a ten pence piece. So I texts our Shantelll and she nips in quietly and slips me one of those foreign Yuros. Clever girl, I thought. Waste not want not.

Dai's bowels are much better. Shantelll had a record played for him last week on Radio Wales: Spencer Davis Band's 'Keep on Running'. She's such a thoughtful girl.

Monday

We're off to bingo today. Oh I loves a game of bingo. Shantelll can mark 48 books, she was always good in school with maths.

Philll is overdoing it a little, there's patients back and fore all times of the day and night. I told him straight, "You'll never keep this up my boy," but he's had no complaints so far. They all come back for more. He must 'ave the magic touch.

I'm just back from sin city. I've been to clean our Philll's apartment in the bay, he's got a lot of clients in Cardiff. It must be a tight squeeze. I overheard him talking about fags on the 'phone, funny, I didn't know that our Philll smoked. Shantelll said he smoulders a bit.

Tuesday

This mansion is getting too big for me to clean so we are advertising for a cleaner and Shantelll's holding auditions today out in the conservatory, God help them. I want someone tidy and not frightened to do a bit of work, none of this stop for a cup of tea every five minutes. I wants tidy mopping not zig zags like they do do up the club, and plenty of pineapple cubes down the bog. Which reminds me, I must lock them away, the dogs keeps eating them.

It's a problem to know what to do for food all time, so I'm trying something new tonight: cheese on toast with bolognaise sauce over it. Oh we're getting so continental lately, what with all these 'olidays and of course the Spaniards who live here as well. Mind you, I love a paella but Dai says paella doesn't 'ave enough chips with it. He'll never learn.

Wednesday

We've decided on a cleaner, her name is Marcia the Merciless, well that's what's on her tattoo on her arm.

We've decided to pay a visit to the Royal Welsh this year. I remember the last time we went, I saw a load of cows and I said to our Shantelll, "Look at those load of cows over there." Shantelll said, "It's alright Mam, I know them, they go to bingo on a Thursday."

Thursday

Marcia is doing well and she's a smart girl to go with it. Her Doctor Martins are always gleaming. She's building a new fireplace for us next week. She's got muscles everywhere, not to mention her party piece where she cracks walnuts in the most ridiculous place. Talented girl, I call her.

One thing I've noticed is the fags she smokes, she rolls her own. God knows why, she gets a good wage. The rolls smell funny but quite pleasant at the end of a hard day. I always gets the giggles when I'm with her.

Friday

A fella came to the door this morning, investigating. Did we 'ave any dope here? I told him straight, "Dai's upstairs."

He soon went when Philll said to him, "Hello again love." When he saw Shantelll he bolted on the double. Shantelll shouted at him, "Remember me to your wife love." We never saw him again.

Philll wants us all to go to the Cannes film festival, perhaps we'll see our Shantelll's film that she made in 'olland. God that was a hard part to play. It's up to Dai if we go or not really as he has to sign on on a Tuesday. We'll 'ave to speak to the Social to see if he can sign on for a month.

Mind you, I'm not fussed. The trouble with France is that they all speaks French over there. Very inconsiderate they are and they all do impressions of Frank Spencer, with tams on their heads. Mind you, this family has got a taste for travelling lately. I fancies a weekend in Merthyr, they do a lovely chips up there and a smashing pint of Dark. After all, if it's good enough for that Owen Money, it's good enough for me. I loves him!!!!!!!!!!!!!

The new Holiday Season
* WEEK 8 *

WELL HELLO MY LOVELIES, how are you this week? We are trying to settle down a bit this week. We've been doing so much travelling lately, what with the Caribbean and the motor home and the boat, well there's only so much you can do on the Social, innit? Anyway, here goes...

Saturday

Our Shantelll has been successful in getting a part-time job in the garden centre in Swansea and she's really looking forward to it as well. She went today in her new uniform, she loves uniforms you know, her favrite being the nurses one. She's always wanted to help people and take them in hand.

Anyway, I gives our Shantelll a sly ring on her mobile and she answers so I says to her, "How's the job going love?" She says to me, "OK Mam, I'm outside at the moment. I'm trimming my bush. It'll look tidy for the weekend in case somebody wants it." Ooh I was relieved.

Sunday

I've let our Shantelll 'ave a lie in this morning, she's done well at the garden centre. Then I went to open the curtains at the back of the house and there's a load of trees and flowers out the back. I thought to myself, Shantelll's been doing a bit of shopping.

Just then our Shantelll popped her head around the door and said, "Do you like the new plants Mam?" I said to her, "How did you get these all home?" She said, "Oh, I had a meeting with the manager, we got on well, especially him. He told me that if I went beyond the call of duty I could 'ave anything I liked." Well, I thought to myself, it's got to be her eyes, people can't resist her eyes and there must 'ave been a grand's worth out the back.

Shantelll's working this afternoon with our Philll, she's got a special client to see to. She said not to disturb her as she'll be tied up all afternoon.

Anyway, time to get our Dai's bit of dinner ready. I never know what time he's gonna pop in and I'm trying to get him to eat healthy, so I've got a salad ready for him. All he's got to do is pop it in the microwave for three minutes, easy love.

Monday

Dai wasn't fussed on that salad yesterday, he's so ungrateful you know. Our Shantelll has got some terrible marks on her back and her legs. I've told her to change that mattress, it's no good for her. That girl's got no way with her. She needs whipping into shape if you ask me.

I never forget the time when Shantelll went for an interview with the army and this sergeant major said to her, "Shantelll, what would you do if you saw a big soldier coming towards you with a big weapon in his hand?" She said, "I'd smile, sir." Mind you, it's a different story with our Philll. He said he could kill a man, eventually.

I feel sorry for our Idwal, there's a woman up the estate after him. Mind you he's a right goer and he was a right boy and a half years ago. I always remember when Idwal was in the forces in Germany. At that time that there was no Yuros, just Marks, and he went out for a night out with this German piece, a lady of horizontal refreshment, if you see what I means. When he had finished his session with her, he was putting his uniform back on and making his way though the door when this German piece said to him, "Idwal, what about the Marks?" Our Idwal said, "Ten out of ten love, ten out of ten."

Tuesday

Shantelll is going to land herself in hot water if she carries on like she is. She keeps talking about that Mark Buckleys from the Chris Needs show. I told her, "He's much too tall for you," but apparently she's gonna park her motor home outside the BBC and wait for him one night. I told her, "Why don't you ask that Chris Needs out? He's nice and respectable." Guess what she told me, she said, "Mam, zip it. I'm fed up, not hard up and I'm certainly not a miracle worker." Well I pops up to see Elsie for coffee and a bit of Jamie Owen and she goes an' puts a load of washing out on the line and six pairs of her knickers. They are massive bloomers and they took flight when the wind got up them. I told our Dai when he came in and he said, "Aw love, bet it was like someone's tent taking off." Mind you, it's about time she had some new ones, the old ones were thread bear, you could see right through them.

Wednesday

Shantelll has given up the job at the garden centre, too much pollen for her sinassess. But she's left on a good note, the manager is coming up to see her soon with a bonus for her. He just can't leave her alone. It's those eyes it is.

We're off out on the boat later on today. Dai wants to try and catch some mackerel. Idwal's not allowed at Swansea marina now after he did a number two on board in the toilet and dumped it in the marina. It's a wonder the fish 'aven't got three eyes down there now, I'm telling you.

Philll's new leather trousers 'ave come, they're from a special place in London but there's a fault with them. There's no seat to them, you can see his bottom clearly. I thought to myself, there's no craftsmanship anymore. I told him straight, "You'll catch a cold wearing those and don't even think of sitting down on a slab or something. You know what will 'appen again, you'll get the chaps."

Our Shantelll 'ave had a new bra that makes you look bigger up top. She tried it on and she asked me, "Mam, what do you think of my lulus?" I told her straight, "I went off her after the Eurovision Song Contest."

Thursday

Our cleaner, Marcia the Merciless, is doing well. She's built a fab fireplace for us, she nicked the bricks from the council.